Criminal Justice Decisions of the United States Supreme Court

Maureen Harrison & Steve Gilbert
Editors

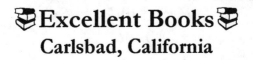

Excellent Books
Carlsbad, California

EXCELLENT BOOKS
Post Office Box 131322
Carlsbad, CA 92013-1322

Copyright © 2003 by Excellent Books. Printed in the U.S.A.

Publisher's Cataloging in Publication Data

Criminal Justice Decisions Of The United States Supreme Court/
 Maureen Harrison, Steve Gilbert, editors.
  p. cm.
Bibliography: p.

1. United States. Supreme Court.
I. Title. II. Harrison, Maureen. III. Gilbert, Steve.

KF4594.C74 2003   LC 98-72976
342.73 -dc20

ISBN 1-880780-15-1

Introduction

You are under arrest. You have the right to remain silent. Any statement you do make may be used as evidence against you. You have the right to consult with an attorney and to have one present during police questioning. If you cannot afford an attorney one will be provided for you. Do you understand your rights? **- The Miranda Warning**

According to the Federal Bureau of Investigation, over 10 million people are arrested in America every year, accused of crimes ranging from murder to loitering. The Bill of Rights, the first ten Amendments to the United States Constitution, provides to all those persons legal protections, among them the right to remain silent, and the right to be represented by legal counsel.

The Fifth Amendment, enacted as part of the Bill of Rights in 1791, provides: *No person shall be compelled in any criminal case to be a witness against himself.* It was not until 1966 that the United States Supreme Court, in the landmark *Miranda* "Right To Remain Silent" Decision, guaranteed to all Americans accused of a crime the right to be "read their rights."

The Sixth Amendment, also enacted as part of the Bill of Rights in 1791, provides: *In all criminal prosecutions the accused shall enjoy the right to have the assistance of counsel for his defense.* It was not until 1964 that the United States Supreme Court, in the landmark *Gideon* "Fair Trial" Decision, guaranteed to all Americans accused of a crime, including those who could not afford it, access to legal counsel.

It is the United States Supreme Court that enunciates the meaning of the Constitution. What is "the right to remain silent"? What is "the right to have assistance of counsel"? Former Chief Justice Charles Evans Hughes summed up the United State Supreme Court's responsibility in this way: *We are under a Constitution, but the Constitution is what the Justices say it is.*

Justice Benjamin Cardozo wrote this about some of the people whose personal legal problems have reached the United States

Supreme Court - *The sordid controversies of litigants are the stuff out of which great and shining truths will ultimately be shaped.* The "sordid controversies" of people charged with criminal activities have many times found their way before the Supreme Court to become the "stuff out of which great and shining truths are shaped." These "great and shining truths," the Supreme Court's decisions on what constitutes criminal justice, have become binding legal precedents - the settled law of the land.

In its long history, the Supreme Court has issued thousands of individual decisions on Constitutional controversies. All have been important to the parties involved, but some - a significant few - are so important as to involve either the Constitutional rights or the Constitutional restrictions placed upon the rights of all Americans. These are Landmark Decisions, fundamentally altering the relationships of Americans to their institutions and to each other. This book deals with landmark decisions on criminal justice.

On the first Monday of each October, the United States Supreme Court begins a new Term. From all over the country, on all kinds of issues, and for all kinds of reasons, Americans bring controversies to the Court for a final disposition. Every year over five thousand requests for review of lower court decisions are received by the Court. Requests, called *petitions for certiorari,* come to the Court from the losing side in Federal Appeals Courts or State Supreme Courts. Four of the nine Justices must agree to a review. Review is accepted in only about four hundred cases each year. Once accepted, written arguments - briefs, pro and con - are submitted to the Court by both the petitioner (the losing side appealing the lower court's decision against them) and the respondent (the winning side defending the lower court's decision for them). Interested parties, called *amici curiae* (friends of the Court), may be permitted to submit briefs in support of either side. After all submitted briefs are reviewed by the Justices, public oral arguments are heard by the Court. Ordinarily the opposing sides, the petitioner and the respondent, are given thirty minutes of oral argument. The Justices, at their discretion, may interrupt at any time to require further explanations, to pose hypothetical questions, or to make observations. Twice a week, on

Wednesdays and Fridays, the Justices meet alone in conference to discuss each case and vote on its outcome. They may affirm [let stand] or reverse [change the outcome of], in whole or in part, the decisions of the lower courts from which these appeals have come. One Justice, voting in the majority, will be selected to write the majority opinion. Others may join in the majority opinion, write their own concurring opinion, write their own dissenting opinion, or join in another's concurrence or dissent. Drafts of the majority, concurring, and dissenting opinions circulate among the Justices, and are redrafted and recirculated until a consensus is reached and a decision is announced. It is the majority opinion as finally issued by the Supreme Court that stands as the law of the land. All other Courts, Federal and State, are bound by Supreme Court precedent. The official legal texts of these decisions are published in the five hundred-plus volumes of *U.S. Reports*.

Judge Learned Hand wrote - *The language of the law must not be foreign to the ears of those who are to obey it*. The Landmark Decisions presented in this book are carefully edited, plain-English versions of the official legal texts issued by the Supreme Court in *United States Reports*. We, as editors, have made every effort to replace esoteric legalese with understandable everyday English without damaging the original decisions. Edited out are long alphanumeric legal citations and wordy wrangles over points of procedure. Edited in are definitions (*writ of habeas corpus* = an order from a judge to bring a person to court), translations (*certiorari* = the decision of the Court to review a case), identifications (petitioner = the individual appealing a lower court's decision; respondent = the individual defending the lower court's decision), and explanations (where the case originated, how it got to the court, and who all the parties involved were).

You will find in *Criminal Justice Decisions* the majority opinion of the Court as expressed by the Justice chosen to speak for the Court. Preceding each edited decision, we note where the complete decision can be found. The bibliography provides a list of further reading on the issues before the Court.

Chief Justice John Marshall wrote that a Supreme Court decision "comes home in its effect to every man's fireside; it passes on his property, his reputation, his life, his all." We entered into editing books on landmark Supreme Court decisions because we, like you, and your family and friends, must obey, under penalty of law, these decisions. It stands to reason that if we owe our obedience to what the Supreme Court decides, then we owe it to ourselves to know what they have written, not second-hand, but for ourselves. You don't have to wait to have your rights read to you - you can read them for yourself.

M.H.& S.G.

Table of Contents

No person shall be "subject for the same offense to be twice put in jeopardy of life or limb." - Justice Benjamin Cardozo (1937)

The essence of a provision forbidding the acquisition of evidence in a certain way is that not merely evidence so acquired shall not be used before the court, but that it shall not be used at all. - Justice Felix Frankfurter (1939)

[T]hey who have suffered most from secret and dictatorial proceedings have almost always been the poor, the ignorant, the numerically weak, the friendless, and the powerless. - Justice Hugo Black (1940)

[I]n the great majority of the states, it has been the considered judgment of the people, their representatives, and their courts that appointment of counsel is not a fundamental right, essential to a fair trial.
- Justice Owen J. Roberts (1942)

The criminal goes free, if he must, but it is the law that sets him free. Nothing can destroy a government more quickly than its failure to observe its own laws, or worse, its disregard of the charter of its own existence.
- Justice Tom Clark (1961)

Indigent Defendants
Gideon v. Wainwright
49

The right of one charged with crime to counsel may not be deemed fundamental and essential to fair trials in some countries, but it is in ours.

— Justice Hugo Black (1963)

The Right To Counsel
Escobedo v. Illinois
59

If the exercise of constitutional rights will thwart the effectiveness of a system of law enforcement, then there is something very wrong with that system.

— Justice Arthur Goldberg (1964)

The Right To Confront Your Accuser
Pointer v. Texas
71

The fact that this right appears in the Sixth Amendment of our Bill of Rights reflects the belief of the Framers of those liberties and safeguards that confrontation was a fundamental right. — Justice Hugo Black (1965)

The Right To Remain Silent
Miranda v. Arizona
79

Prior to any questioning, the person must be warned that he has a right to remain silent, that any statement he does make may be used as evidence against him, and that he has a right to the presence of an attorney.

— Chief Justice Earl Warren (1966)

Preventive Detention
United States v. Salerno
95

[T]he Government may detain individuals whom the Government believes to be dangerous. — Chief Justice William Rehnquist (1987)

Double Jeopardy
Palko v. Connecticut

No person shall be subject for the same offense to be twice put in jeopardy of life or limb.   - **The Double Jeopardy Clause**

No State shall deprive any person of life, liberty, or property without due process of law.   - **The Due Process Clause**

Frank Palko was tried for murder in Connecticut's Fairfield County Superior Court. The judge, over the objection of State prosecutors, excluded testimony that Palko had confessed to the crime. Prosecutors asked the jury to find Palko guilty of first degree murder - a sentence that carried the death penalty. The jury, based on the evidence that they had heard, found Palko guilty of second-degree murder - a sentence that carried life imprisonment.

The State, under an 1886 Connecticut law that gave prosecutors the same rights of appeal as those given to persons convicted of a crime, petitioned Connecticut's Supreme Court of Errors to reverse the second-degree murder conviction and order a new trial in which Palko's excluded confession would be admitted into testimony.

Palko argued that to put him on trial a second time for a crime for which he had already been convicted, would violate his Fifth Amendment right against double jeopardy and his Fourteenth Amendment right to due process. Connecticut's Supreme Court of Errors rejected Palko's argument and ordered a second trial. With the testimony of his confession admitted into evidence, a second jury found Palko guilty of first-degree murder and sentenced him to death. Palko appealed to the United States Supreme Court.

On December 6, 1937 the 8-1 decision of the United States Supreme Court was announced by Associate Justice Benjamin Cardozo.

The *Palko* Court

Chief Justice Charles Evans Hughes
Appointed Associate Justice by President Taft
Appointed Chief Justice by President Hoover
Served 1910 - 1916, 1930 -1941

Associate Justice James McReynolds
Appointed by President Wilson
Served 1914 - 1941

Associate Justice Louis Brandeis
Appointed by President Wilson
Served 1916 - 1939

Associate Justice George Sutherland
Appointed by President Harding
Served 1922 - 1938

Associate Justice Pierce Butler
Appointed by President Harding
Served 1922 - 1939

Associate Justice Harlan Fiske Stone
Appointed by President Coolidge
Served 1925 - 1946

Associate Justice Owen Roberts
Appointed by President Hoover
Served 1930 - 1945

Associate Justice Benjamin Cardozo
Appointed by President Hoover
Served 1932 - 1938

Associate Justice Hugo Black
Appointed by President Franklin Roosevelt
Served 1937 - 1971

The legal text of *Palko v. Connecticut* can be found in volume 302 of *United States Reports*. Our edited text follows.

PALKO v. CONNECTICUT
December 6, 1937

JUSTICE BENJAMIN CARDOZO: A statute of Connecticut permitting appeals in criminal cases to be taken by the state is challenged by appellant [person appealing to the court, Frank Palko] as an infringement of the Fourteenth Amendment of the Constitution of the United States. Whether the challenge should be upheld is now to be determined.

[Palko] was indicted [charged] in Fairfield County, Connecticut, for the crime of murder in the first degree. A jury found him guilty of murder in the second degree, and he was sentenced to confinement in the state prison for life. Thereafter, the State of Connecticut . . . appeal[ed] to the Supreme Court of Errors. This it did pursuant to an act adopted in 1886. . . . Upon such appeal, the Supreme Court of Errors reversed the judgment and ordered a new trial. It found that there had been error of law to the prejudice of the state (1) in excluding testimony as to a confession by defendant [person accused of wrongdoing]; (2) in excluding testimony upon cross-examination of defendant to impeach his credibility, and (3) in the instructions to the jury as to the difference between first and second degree murder.

Pursuant to the mandate of the Supreme Court of Errors, [Palko] was brought to trial again. Before a jury was impaneled and also at later stages of the case, he made the objection that the effect of the new trial was to place him twice in jeopardy for the same offense, and, in so doing, to violate the Fourteenth Amendment of the Constitution of the United States. Upon the overruling of the objection, the trial proceeded. The jury returned a verdict of murder in the first degree, and the court sentenced [Palko] to the punishment of death. The Supreme Court of Errors affirmed [upheld] the judgment of conviction, adhering to a decision announced in 1894, which upheld the challenged statute. The case is here upon appeal.

The execution of the sentence will not deprive [Palko] of his life without the process of law assured to him by the Fourteenth Amendment of the Federal Constitution.

The argument for [Palko] is that whatever is forbidden by the Fifth Amendment is forbidden by the Fourteenth also. The Fifth Amendment, which is not directed to the states, but solely to the federal government, creates immunity from double jeopardy. No person shall be "subject for the same offense to be twice put in jeopardy of life or limb." The Fourteenth Amendment ordains, "nor shall any State deprive any person of life, liberty, or property, without due process of law." To retry a defendant, though under one indictment and only one, subjects him, it is said, to double jeopardy in violation of the Fifth Amendment, if the prosecution is one on behalf of the United States. From this the consequence is said to follow that there is a denial of life or liberty without due process of law, if the prosecution is one on behalf of the People of a State. . . . The question is now here.

We do not find it profitable to mark the precise limits of the prohibition of double jeopardy in federal prosecutions. The subject was much considered in *Kepner v. United States*, decided in 1904 by a closely divided court. The view was there expressed for a majority of the court that the prohibition was not confined to jeopardy in a new and independent case. It forbade jeopardy in the same case if the new trial was at the instance of the government, and not upon defendant's motion. All this may be assumed for the purpose of the case at hand, though the dissenting opinions show how much was to be said in favor of a different ruling. Right-minded men, as we learn from those opinions, could reasonably, even if mistakenly, believe that a second trial was lawful in prosecutions subject to the Fifth Amendment, if it was all in the same case. Even more plainly, right-minded men could reasonably believe that in espousing that conclusion they were not favoring a practice repugnant to the conscience of mankind. Is double jeopardy in such circumstances, if double jeopardy it must be called, a denial of due process forbidden to the States? The tyranny of labels must not lead us to leap to a conclusion that a word which in one set of facts may stand for oppression or enormity is of like effect in every other.

We have said that in [Palko]'s view the Fourteenth Amendment is to be taken as embodying the prohibitions of the Fifth. His thesis is even broader. Whatever would be a violation of the original bill of rights (Amendments I to VIII) if done by the federal government is now equally unlawful by force of the Fourteenth Amendment if done by a state. There is no such general rule.

The Fifth Amendment provides, among other things, that no person shall be held to answer for a capital [one punishable by the death penalty] or otherwise infamous crime unless on presentment [accusation] or indictment of a grand jury. This court has held that, in prosecutions by a state, presentment or indictment by a grand jury may give way to informations [charges similar to indictments] at the instance of a public officer. The Fifth Amendment provides also that no person shall be compelled in any criminal case to be a witness against himself. This court has said that, in prosecutions by a State, the exemption will fail if the State elects to end it. The Sixth Amendment calls for a jury trial in criminal cases and the Seventh for a jury trial in civil cases at common law where the value in controversy shall exceed twenty dollars. This court has ruled that consistently with those amendments trial by jury may be modified by a state or abolished altogether. . . .

On the other hand, the due process clause of the Fourteenth Amendment may make it unlawful for a State to abridge by its statutes the freedom of speech which the First Amendment safeguards against encroachment by the Congress, or the like freedom of the press, or the free exercise of religion, or the right of peaceable assembly, without which speech would be unduly trammeled, or the right of one accused of crime to the benefit of counsel. In these and other situations immunities that are valid as against the federal government by force of the specific pledges of particular amendments have been found to be implicit in the concept of ordered liberty, and thus, through the Fourteenth Amendment, become valid as against the States.

The line of division may seem to be wavering and broken if there is a hasty catalog of the cases on the one side and the other. Reflection and analysis will induce a different view. There emerges the perception of a rationalizing principle which gives to discrete instances a proper order and coherence. The right to trial by jury and the immunity from prosecution except as the result of an indictment may have value and importance. Even so, they are not of the very essence of a scheme of ordered liberty. To abolish them is not to violate a "principle of justice so rooted in the traditions and conscience of our people as to be ranked as fundamental." Few would be so narrow or provincial as to maintain that a fair and enlightened system of justice would be impossible without them. What is true of jury trials and indictments is true also, as the cases show, of the immunity from compulsory self-incrimination. This too might be lost, and justice still be done. Indeed, today as in the past there are students of our penal system who look upon the immunity as a mischief rather than a benefit, and who would limit its scope or destroy it altogether. No doubt there would remain the need to give protection against torture, physical or mental. Justice, however, would not perish if the accused were subject to a duty to respond to orderly inquiry. The exclusion of these immunities and privileges from the privileges and immunities protected against the action of the States has not been arbitrary or casual. It has been dictated by a study and appreciation of the meaning, the essential implications, of liberty itself.

We reach a different plane of social and moral values when we pass to the privileges and immunities that have been taken over from the earlier articles of the federal Bill of Rights and brought within the Fourteenth Amendment by a process of absorption. These in their origin were effective against the federal government alone. If the Fourteenth Amendment has absorbed them, the process of absorption has had its source in the belief that neither liberty nor justice would exist if they were sacrificed. This is true, for illustration, of freedom of thought and speech. Of that freedom one may say that it is the matrix, the indispensable condition, of nearly every other form of freedom. With rare aberrations, a pervasive recognition of that truth can be traced in our history, political and legal. So it has come about that the domain of liberty, withdrawn by the Fourteenth Amendment from encroachment by the States, has been enlarged by latter-day judgments to include liberty of the mind as well as liberty of action. The extension became, indeed, a logical imperative when once it was recognized, as long ago it was, that liberty is something more than exemption from physical restraint, and that even in the field of substantive rights and duties the legislative judgment, if oppressive and arbitrary, may be overridden by the courts. Fundamental too in the concept of due process, and so in that of liberty, is the thought that condemnation shall be rendered only after trial. The hearing, moreover, must be a real one, not a sham or a pretense. For that reason, ignorant defendants in a capital case were held to have been condemned unlawfully when in truth, though not in form, they were refused the aid of counsel. The decision did not turn upon the fact that the benefit of counsel would have been guaranteed to the defendants by the provisions of the Sixth Amendment if they had been prosecuted in a federal court. The decision turned upon the fact that in the particular situation laid before us in the evidence the benefit of counsel was essential to the substance of a hearing.

Our survey of the cases serves, we think, to justify the statement that the dividing line between them, if not unfaltering throughout its course, has been true for the most part to a unifying principle. On which side of the line the case made out by [Palko] has appropriate location must be the next inquiry, and the final one. Is that kind of double jeopardy to which the statute has subjected him a hardship so acute and shocking that our polity [form of government] will not endure it? Does it violate those "fundamental principles of liberty and justice which lie at the base of all our civil and political institutions?" The answer surely must be "no." What the answer would have to be if the state were permitted after a trial free from error to try the accused over again or to bring another case against him, we have no occasion to consider. We deal with the statute before us and no other. The State is not attempting to wear the accused out by a multitude of cases with accumulated trials. It asks no more than this, that the case against him shall go on until there shall be a trial free from the corrosion of substantial legal error. This is not cruelty at all, nor even vexation in any immoderate degree. If the trial had been infected with error adverse to the accused, there might have been review at his instance, and as often as necessary to purge the vicious taint. A reciprocal privilege, subject at all times to the discretion of the presiding judge, has now been granted to the State. There is here no seismic innovation. The edifice of justice stands, in its symmetry, to many, greater than before.

The conviction of [Palko] is not in derogation of any privileges or immunities that belong to him as a citizen of the United States. There is argument in his behalf that the privileges and immunities clause of the Fourteenth Amendment as well as the due process clause has been flouted by the judgment.

The judgment is affirmed.

The Fruit Of The Poisonous Tree
Nardone v. United States

On January 16, 1919 the ratification of the Constitution's Eighteenth Amendment, the Prohibition Amendment, made the importation of "intoxicating liquors" into the United States a Federal crime.

On March 17, 1936 United States Treasury Agents, acting on information they had obtained from secretly recorded telephone conversations, "taps" for which they had not obtained a court order, raided a ship in New York Harbor loaded with illegally imported alcohol. Frank Carmine Nardone, charged by the Federal Government with being the ringleader of the bootlegging gang responsible for the illegal shipment, was arrested for conspiracy to smuggle alcohol into the United States. Tried in United States District Court, Nardone was convicted, based largely on the incriminating evidence obtained by the Government from their "tap" on his telephone.

Nardone appealed his conviction to the United States Court of Appeals, arguing that the Federal Government's wiretap evidence was obtained illegally and so was "tainted" evidence which should have been excluded from his trial as a violation of both the Fourth Amendment's prohibition against unreasonable searches and seizures and the Fifth Amendment's prohibition against self-incrimination. On July 20, 1939 the U.S. Court of Appeals rejected Nardone's argument and affirmed his conviction. Nardone appealed for a final determination to the U.S. Supreme Court.

On December 11, 1939 the 7-1 decision of the U.S. Supreme Court was announced by Associate Justice Felix Frankfurter.

The *Nardone* Court

Chief Justice Harlan Fiske Stone
Appointed Associate Justice by President Coolidge
Appointed Chief Justice by President Franklin Roosevelt
Served 1925 - 1946

Associate Justice Owen Roberts
Appointed by President Hoover
Served 1930 - 1945

Associate Justice Hugo Black
Appointed by President Franklin Roosevelt
Served 1937 - 1971

Associate Justice Felix Frankfurter
Appointed by President Franklin Roosevelt
Served 1939 - 1962

Associate Justice William Douglas
Appointed by President Franklin Roosevelt
Served 1939 - 1975

Associate Justice Francis Murphy
Appointed by President Franklin Roosevelt
Served 1940 - 1949

Associate Justice James Byrnes
Appointed by President Franklin Roosevelt
Served 1941 - 1942

Associate Justice Robert Jackson
Appointed by President Franklin Roosevelt
Served 1941 - 1954

The legal text of *Nardone v. U.S.* can be found in volume 302 of
United States Reports. Our edited text follows.

NARDONE v. UNITED STATES
December 11, 1939

JUSTICE FELIX FRANKFURTER: We are called upon for the
second time to review . . . petitioners' [Nardone's and others']
convictions under an indictment [a charge] for frauds on the
revenue. . . . [We] reversed the convictions on the first trial because they were procured by evidence secured in violation of
Section 605 of the Communications Act of 1934. . . . [T]his evidence consisted of intercepted telephone messages, constituting
"a vital part of the prosecution's proof."

Conviction followed a new trial, and "the main question" on the
appeal [in the lower court] is the only question open here -
namely, "whether the [trial] judge improperly refused to allow the
accused to examine the prosecution as to the uses to which it had
put the information" which *Nardone v. United States* found to have
vitiated [voided] the original conviction. Though candidly doubtful of the result it reached, the Circuit Court of Appeals . . . ruled
that "Congress had not also made incompetent testimony which
had become accessible by the use of unlawful 'taps,' for to divulge that information was not to divulge an intercepted telephone talk."

The issue thus tendered by the Circuit Court of Appeals is the
broad one, whether . . . Section 605 merely interdicts [prohibits]
the introduction into evidence in a federal trial of intercepted
telephone conversations, leaving the prosecution free to make
every other use of the proscribed [prohibited] evidence. Plainly,
this presents a far-reaching problem in the administration of federal criminal justice, and we therefore brought the case here for
disposition.

Any claim for the exclusion of evidence logically relevant in criminal prosecutions is heavily handicapped. It must be justified by
an overriding public policy expressed in the Constitution or the
law of the land. In a problem such as that before us now, two
opposing concerns must be harmonized: on the one hand, the
stern enforcement of the criminal law; on the other, protection of

that realm of privacy left free by Constitution and laws but capable of infringement either through zeal or design. In accomodating both these concerns, meaning must be given to what Congress has written, even if not in explicit language, so as to effectuate the policy which Congress has formulated.

We are here dealing with specific prohibition of particular methods in obtaining evidence. The result of the holding [of the lower court] is to reduce the scope of Section 605 to exclusion of the exact words heard through forbidden interceptions, allowing these interceptions every derivative use that they may serve. Such a reading . . . would largely stultify the policy which compelled our decision in *Nardone v. United States*. That decision was not the product of a merely meticulous reading of technical language. It was the translation into practicality of broad considerations of morality and public well-being. This Court found that the logically relevant proof which Congress had outlawed, it outlawed because "inconsistent with ethical standards and destructive of personal liberty." To forbid the direct use of methods thus characterized but to put no curb on their full indirect use would only invite the very methods deemed "inconsistent with ethical standards and destructive of personal liberty." What was said in a different context in *Silverthorne Lumber Co. v. United States* is pertinent here, "The essence of a provision forbidding the acquisition of evidence in a certain way is that not merely evidence so acquired shall not be used before the court, but that it shall not be used at all." A decent respect for the policy of Congress must save us from imputing to it a self-defeating, if not disingenuous purpose.

Here, as in the *Silverthorne* Case, the facts improperly obtained do not "become sacred and inaccessible. If knowledge of them is gained from an independent source they may be proved like any others, but the knowledge gained by the Government's own wrong cannot be used by it" simply because it is used derivatively.

In practice this generalized statement may conceal concrete complexities. Sophisticated argument may prove a causal connection between information obtained through illicit wiretapping and the

Government's proof. As a matter of good sense, however, such connection may have become so attenuated as to dissipate the taint. A sensible way of dealing with such a situation - fair to the intendment of Section 605, but fair also to the purposes of the criminal law - ought to be within the reach of experienced trial judges. The burden is, of course, on the accused in the first instance to prove to the trial court's satisfaction that wire-tapping was unlawfully employed. Once that is established - as was plainly done here - the trial judge must give opportunity, however closely confined, to the accused to prove that a substantial portion of the case against him was a fruit of the poisonous tree. This leaves ample opportunity to the Government to convince the trial court that its proof had an independent origin.

Dispatch in the trial of criminal causes is essential in bringing crime to book. Therefore, timely steps must be taken to secure judicial determination of claims of illegality on the part of agents of the Government in obtaining testimony. To interrupt the course of the trial for such auxiliary inquiries impedes the momentum of the main proceeding and breaks the continuity of the jury's attention. Like mischief would result were tenuous claims sufficient to justify the trial court's indulgence of inquiry into the legitimacy of evidence in the Government's possession. So to read a congressional prohibition against the availability of certain evidence would be to subordinate the need for rigorous administration of justice to undue solicitude for potential and, it is to be hoped, abnormal disobedience of the law by the law's officers. Therefore claims that taint attaches to any portion of the Government's case must satisfy the trial court with their solidity and not be merely a means of eliciting what is in the Government's possession before its submission to the jury. And if such a claim is made after the trial is under way, the judge must likewise be satisfied that the accused could not at an earlier stage have had adequate knowledge to make his claim. The civilized conduct of criminal trials cannot be confined within mechanical rules. It necessarily demands the authority of limited direction entrusted to the judge presiding in federal trials, including a well-established range of judicial discretion, subject to appropriate review on appeal, in ruling upon preliminary questions of fact. Such a system as ours must, within the limits here indicated, rely on the learning, good sense, fairness and courage of federal trial judges.

We have dealt with this case on the basic issue tendered by the Circuit Court of Appeals and have not indulged in a finicking appraisal of the record, either as to the issue of the time limit of the proposed inquiry into the use to which the Government had put its illicit practices, or as to the existence of independent sources for the Government's proof. Since the Circuit Court of Appeals did not question its timeliness, we shall not. And the hostility of the trial court to the whole scope of the inquiry reflected his own accord with the rule of law by which the Circuit Court of Appeals sustained [upheld] him, and which we find erroneous.

The judgment must be reversed and remanded [returned] to the District Court for further proceedings in conformity with this opinion.

Coerced Confessions
Chambers v. Florida

On Friday night, May 13, 1933, in Pompano, Florida, an elderly white man was murdered. Between May 13 and 14 several dozen African-Americans were illegally detained and questioned by Broward County police. Suspicion finally settled on four men - Jack Williamson, Charlie Davis, Walter Woodward, and Isaiah Chambers.

From Sunday, May 14 through early Saturday, May 20, the four were repeatedly questioned. The police later described their on-and-off questioning as the standard "third degree." From late Saturday, May 20 until early Sunday, May 21, the four were unrelentingly questioned all day and night. The four would later describe their continuous questioning as "terrifying and violent." After five days and nights, all four signed "voluntary" confessions. Indicted for murder on Monday, May 21, Williamson, Davis, and Woodward pled guilty. Chambers, who repudiated his confession as having been coerced from him through force and fear, pled innocent.

Chambers was tried for murder in Palm Beach County Circuit Court (the trial having been moved from Broward County) and, based on his "confession," was convicted and, like the others, sentenced to death. Chambers appealed his conviction to the Florida Supreme Court, arguing that his confession had been illegally obtained by police coercion in violation of the Due Process Clause of the Fourteenth Amendment. The Florida Supreme Court upheld his death sentence. Chambers appealed for a final determination to the United States Supreme Court.

On February 12, 1940 the 8-0 decision of the U.S. Supreme Court was announced by Associate Justice Hugo Black.

The *Chambers* Court

Chief Justice Charles Evans Hughes
Appointed Associate Justice by President Taft
Appointed Chief Justice by President Hoover
Served 1910 - 1916, 1930 -1941

Associate Justice James McReynolds
Appointed by President Wilson
Served 1914 - 1941

Associate Justice Harlan Fiske Stone
Appointed by President Coolidge
Served 1925 - 1946

Associate Justice Owen Roberts
Appointed by President Hoover
Served 1930 - 1945

Associate Justice Hugo Black
Appointed by President Franklin Roosevelt
Served 1937 - 1971

Associate Justice Stanley Reed
Appointed by President Franklin Roosevelt
Served 1938 - 1957

Associate Justice Felix Frankfurter
Appointed by President Franklin Roosevelt
Served 1939 - 1962

Associate Justice William Douglas
Appointed by President Franklin Roosevelt
Served 1939 - 1975

The legal text of *Chambers v. Florida* can be found in volume 309 of *United States Reports*. Our edited text follows.

CHAMBERS v. FLORIDA
February 12, 1940

JUSTICE HUGO BLACK: The grave question presented [here] . . . is whether proceedings in which confessions were utilized, and which culminated in sentences of death upon four young negro men in the State of Florida [Chambers and others], failed to afford the safeguard of that due process of law guaranteed by the Fourteenth Amendment.

First. The State of Florida challenges our [authority to rule on this issue], claiming that . . . due process was [served] . . . because passed upon by a jury. However, use by a State of an improperly obtained confession may constitute a denial of due process of law as guaranteed in the Fourteenth Amendment. Since petitioners [those bringing a case to court] have seasonably asserted the right under the federal Constitution to have their guilt or innocence of a capital crime determined without reliance upon confessions obtained by means proscribed [prohibited] by the Due Process Clause of the Fourteenth Amendment, we must determine independently whether petitioners' confessions were so obtained. . . .

Second. The record shows - About nine o'clock on the night of Saturday, May 13, 1933, Robert Darsey, an elderly white man, was robbed and murdered in Pompano, Florida, a small town in Broward County about twelve miles from Fort Lauderdale, the County seat. The opinion of the Supreme Court of Florida affirming [upholding] petitioners' conviction for this crime stated that, "It was one of those crimes that induced an enraged community. . . ." And, as the dissenting judge pointed out,

"The murder and robbery of the elderly Mr. Darsey . . . was a most dastardly and atrocious crime. It naturally aroused great and well-justified public indignation."

Between 9:30 and 10 o'clock after the murder, petitioner Charlie Davis was arrested, and within the next twenty-four hours from twenty-five to forty negroes living in the community, including petitioners Williamson, Chambers, and Woodward, were arrested without warrants [written orders] and confined in the Broward County jail, at Fort Lauderdale. On the night of the crime, attempts to trail the murderers by bloodhounds brought J. T. Williams, a convict guard, into the proceedings. From then until confessions were obtained and petitioners were sentenced, he took a prominent part. About 11 p.m. on the following Monday, May 15, the sheriff and Williams took several of the imprisoned negroes, including Williamson and Chambers, to the Dade County jail at Miami. The sheriff testified that they were taken there because he felt a possibility of mob violence, and "wanted to give protection to every prisoner . . . in jail." Evidence of petitioners was that on the way to Miami a motorcycle patrolman drew up to the car in which the men were riding and the sheriff "told the cop that he had some negroes that he [was] taking down to Miami to escape a mob." This statement was not denied by the sheriff in his testimony, and Williams did not testify at all; Williams apparently has now disappeared. Upon order of Williams, petitioner Williamson was kept in the death cell of the Dade County jail. The prisoners thus spirited to Miami were returned to the Fort Lauderdale jail the next day, Tuesday.

It is clear from the evidence of both the State and petitioners that from Sunday, May 14, to Saturday, May 20, the thirty to forty negro suspects were subjected to questioning and cross-questioning (with the exception that several of the suspects were in Dade County jail over one night). From the afternoon of Saturday, May 20, until sunrise of the 21st, petitioners and possibly one or two others underwent persistent and repeated questioning. The Supreme Court of Florida said the questioning "was in progress several days and all night before the confessions were secured," and referred to the last night as an "all night vigil." The sheriff who supervised the procedure of continued interrogation testified that he questioned the prisoners "in the day time all the week," but did not question them during any night before the all-night vigil of Saturday, May 20, because after having "questioned them all day . . . [he] was tired." Other evidence of the State was "that the officers of Broward County were in that jail almost continually during the whole week questioning these boys, and other boys, in connection with this" case.

The process of repeated questioning took place in the jailer's quarters on the fourth floor of the jail. During the week following their arrest and until their confessions were finally acceptable to the State's Attorney in the early dawn of Sunday, May 21st, petitioners and their fellow prisoners were led one at a time from their cells to the questioning room, quizzed, and returned to their cells to await another turn. So far as appears, the prisoners at no time during the week were permitted to see or confer with counsel or a single friend or relative. When carried singly from his cell and subjected to questioning, each found himself, a single prisoner, surrounded in a fourth floor jail room by four to ten men, the county sheriff, his deputies, a convict guard, and other white officers and citizens of the community.

The testimony is in conflict as to whether all four petitioners were continually threatened and physically mistreated until they finally, in hopeless desperation and fear of their lives, agreed to confess on Sunday morning just after daylight. Be that as it may, it is certain that by Saturday, May 20th, five days of continued questioning had elicited no confession. Admittedly, a concentration of effort - directed against a small number of prisoners including petitioners - on the part of the questioners, principally the sheriff and Williams, the convict guard, began about 3:30 that Saturday afternoon. From that hour on, with only short intervals for food and rest for the questioners - "They all stayed up all night." "They bring one of them at a time backwards and forwards . . . until they confessed." And Williams was present and participating that night, during the whole of which the jail cook served coffee and sandwiches to the men who "grilled" the prisoners.

Sometime in the early hours of Sunday, the 21st, probably about 2:30 a.m., Woodward apparently "broke"- as one of the State's witnesses put it - after a fifteen or twenty minute period of questioning by Williams, the sheriff and the constable "one right after the other." The State's Attorney was awakened at his home, and called to the jail. He came, but was dissatisfied with the confession of Woodward which he took down in writing at that time, and said something like "tear this paper up, that isn't what I want, when you get something worthwhile call me." This same

State's Attorney conducted the state's case in the circuit court below and also made himself a witness, but did not testify as to why Woodward's first alleged confession was unsatisfactory to him. . . .

Just before sunrise, the state officials got something "worthwhile" from petitioners which the State's Attorney would "want"; again he was called; he came; in the presence of those who had carried on and witnessed the all-night questioning, he caused his questions and petitioners' answers to be stenographically reported. These are the confessions utilized by the State to obtain the judgments upon which petitioners were sentenced to death. No formal charges had been brought before the confessions. Two days thereafter, petitioners were indicted [charged], were arraigned [brought into court to plead guilty or innocent], and Williamson and Woodward pleaded guilty; Chambers and Davis pleaded not guilty. Later the sheriff, accompanied by Williams, informed an attorney who presumably had been appointed to defend Davis that Davis wanted his plea of not guilty withdrawn. This was done, and Davis then pleaded guilty. When Chambers was tried, his conviction rested upon his confession and testimony of the other three confessors. The convict guard and the sheriff "were in the Court room sitting down in a seat." And from arrest until sentenced to death, petitioners were never - either in jail or in court - wholly removed from the constant observation, influence, custody and control of those whose persistent pressure brought about the sunrise confessions.

Third. The scope and operation of the Fourteenth Amendment have been fruitful sources of controversy in our constitutional history. However, in view of its historical setting and the wrongs which called it into being, the Due Process provision of the Fourteenth Amendment - just as that, in the Fifth - has led few to doubt that it was intended to guarantee procedural standards adequate and appropriate, then and thereafter, to protect, at all times, people charged with or suspected of crime by those holding positions of power and authority. Tyrannical governments had immemorially utilized dictatorial criminal procedure and punishment to make scapegoats of the weak, or of helpless political, religious, or racial minorities and those who differed, who would not conform and who resisted tyranny. The instruments of such governments were, in the main, two. Conduct, innocent when engaged in, was subsequently made by fiat criminally punishable without legislation. And a liberty-loving people won the principle that criminal punishments could not be inflicted save for that which proper legislative action had already by "the law of the land" forbidden when done. But even more was needed. From the popular hatred and abhorrence of illegal confinement, torture and extortion of confessions of violations of the "law of the land" evolved the fundamental idea that no man's life, liberty or property be forfeited as criminal punishment for violation of that law until there had been a charge fairly made and fairly tried in a public tribunal free of prejudice, passion, excitement, and tyrannical power. Thus, as assurance against ancient evils, our country, in order to preserve "the blessings of liberty," wrote into its basic law the requirement, among others, that the forfeiture of the lives, liberties or property of people accused of crime can only follow if procedural safeguards of due process have been obeyed.

The determination to preserve an accused's right to procedural due process sprang in large part from knowledge of the historical truth that the rights and liberties of people accused of crime could not be safely entrusted to secret inquisitorial processes. The testimony of centuries, in governments of varying kinds over populations of different races and beliefs, stood as proof that physical and mental torture and coercion had brought about the tragically unjust sacrifices of some who were the noblest and most useful of their generations. The rack, the thumbscrew, the wheel, solitary confinement, protracted questioning and cross-questioning, and other ingenious forms of entrapment of the helpless or unpopular had left their wake of mutilated bodies and shattered minds along the way to the cross, the guillotine, the stake and the hangman's noose. And they who have suffered most from secret and dictatorial proceedings have almost always been the poor, the ignorant, the numerically weak, the friendless, and the powerless.

This requirement - of conforming to fundamental standards of procedure in criminal trials - was made operative against the

States by the Fourteenth Amendment. Where one of several accused had limped into the trial court as a result of admitted
physical mistreatment inflicted to obtain confessions upon which
a jury had returned a verdict of guilty of murder, this Court recently declared, [in] *Brown v. Mississippi*, that, "It would be difficult
to conceive of methods more revolting to the sense of justice
than those taken to procure the confessions of these petitioners,
and the use of the confessions thus obtained as the basis for
conviction and sentence was a clear denial of due process."

Here, the record develops a sharp conflict upon the issue of
physical violence and mistreatment, but shows, without conflict,
the dragnet methods of arrest on suspicion without warrant, and
the protracted questioning and cross-questioning of these ignorant young colored tenant farmers by State officers and other
white citizens, in a fourth floor jail room, where as prisoners they
were without friends, advisers or counselors, and under circumstances calculated to break the strongest nerves and the stoutest
resistance. Just as our decision in *Brown v. Mississippi* was based
upon the fact that the confessions were the result of compulsion,
so in the present case, the admitted practices were such as to justify the statement that, "The undisputed facts showed that compulsion was applied."

For five days, petitioners were subjected to interrogations
culminating in Saturday's (May 20th) all-night examination. Over
a period of five days, they steadily refused to confess, and
disclaimed any guilt. The very circumstances surrounding their
confinement and their questioning, without any formal charges
having been brought, were such as to fill petitioners with terror
and frightful misgivings. Some were practical strangers in the
community; three were arrested in a one-room farm tenant house
which was their home; the haunting fear of mob violence was
around them in an atmosphere charged with excitement and
public indignation. From virtually the moment of their arrest
until their eventual confessions, they never knew just when
anyone would be called back to the fourth floor room, and there,
surrounded by his accusers and others, interrogated by men who
held their very lives - so far as these ignorant petitioners could
know - in the balance. The rejection of petitioner Woodward's

first "confession," given in the early hours of Sunday morning, because it was found wanting, demonstrates the relentless tenacity which "broke" petitioners' will and rendered them helpless to resist their accusers further. To permit human lives to be forfeited upon confessions thus obtained would make of the constitutional requirement of due process of law a meaningless symbol.

We are not impressed by the argument that law enforcement methods such as those under review are necessary to uphold our laws. The Constitution proscribes such lawless means irrespective of the end. And this argument flouts the basic principle that all people must stand on an equality before the bar of justice in every American court. Today, as in ages past, we are not without tragic proof that the exalted power of some governments to punish manufactured crime dictatorially is the handmaid of tyranny. Under our constitutional system, courts stand against any winds that blow as havens of refuge for those who might otherwise suffer because they are helpless, weak, outnumbered, or because they are nonconforming victims of prejudice and public excitement. Due process of law, preserved for all by our Constitution, commands that no such practice as that disclosed by this record shall send any accused to his death. No higher duty, no more solemn responsibility, rests upon this Court, than that of translating into living law and maintaining this constitutional shield deliberately planned and inscribed for the benefit of every human being subject to our Constitution - of whatever race, creed, or persuasion.

The Supreme Court of Florida was in error and its judgment is reversed.

The Fundamental Right To A Fair Trial
Betts v. Brady

In all criminal prosecutions, the accused shall have the assistance of counsel for his defense. **- The Sixth Amendment**

No State shall deprive any person of life, liberty, or property without due process of law. **- The Fourteenth Amendment**

On December 24, 1938 a masked man robbed a grocery store in Carol County, Maryland, stealing $50. An unemployed laborer, Smith Betts, was charged with the crime. Betts, with no money to hire a lawyer, requested that the Carol County Circuit Court appoint one for him. The trial judge denied this request on the grounds that only poor defendants on trial for rape or murder were entitled to a court-appointed lawyer. Betts, without a lawyer to defend him, pled not guilty and attempted to defend himself. Found guilty of armed robbery, Betts was sentenced to eight years' imprisonment.

In 1941 Betts, arguing that he had not received a fair trial, filed a petition with the Chief Judge of the Maryland Court of Appeals, demanding that he be released from the custody of Patrick Brady, Warden of the State Penitentiary. Betts' petition complained that his right to the assistance of counsel, as guaranteed by the Sixth Amendment, and his right to due process of law, as guaranteed by the Fourteenth Amendment, had been violated by the trial judge's refusal to appoint him a lawyer.

The Chief Judge of the Maryland Court of Appeals denied Betts' petition on the grounds that even without a lawyer Betts had received a fair trial. Smith Betts appealed for a final determination to the United States Supreme Court.

On June 1, 1942 the 6-3 decision of the United States Supreme Court was announced by Associate Justice Owen Roberts.

The *Betts* Court

Chief Justice Harlan Fiske Stone
Appointed Associate Justice by President Coolidge
Appointed Chief Justice by President Franklin Roosevelt
Served 1925 - 1946

Associate Justice Owen Roberts
Appointed by President Hoover
Served 1930 - 1945

Associate Justice Hugo Black
Appointed by President Franklin Roosevelt
Served 1937 - 1971

Associate Justice Stanley Reed
Appointed by President Franklin Roosevelt
Served 1938 - 1957

Associate Justice Felix Frankfurter
Appointed by President Franklin Roosevelt
Served 1939 - 1962

Associate Justice William Douglas
Appointed by President Franklin Roosevelt
Served 1939 - 1975

Associate Justice Francis Murphy
Appointed by President Franklin Roosevelt
Served 1940 - 1949

Associate Justice James Byrnes
Appointed by President Franklin Roosevelt
Served 1941 - 1942

Associate Justice Robert Jackson
Appointed by President Franklin Roosevelt
Served 1941 - 1954

The legal text of *Betts v. Brady* can be found in volume 316 of *United States Reports*. Our edited text follows.

BETTS *v.* BRADY
June 1, 1942

JUSTICE OWEN J. ROBERTS: The petitioner [Smith Betts] was indicted for [charged with] robbery in the Circuit Court of Carroll County, Maryland. Due to lack of funds, he was unable to employ counsel, and so informed the judge at his arraignment [court appearance at which one enters a plea of guilty or innocent]. He requested that counsel be appointed for him. The judge advised him that this would not be done as it was not the practice in Carroll County to appoint counsel for indigent defendants save in prosecutions for murder and rape.

Without waiving his asserted right to counsel [Betts] pleaded not guilty and elected to be tried without a jury. At his request witnesses were summoned in his behalf. He cross-examined the State's witnesses and examined his own. The latter gave testimony tending to establish an alibi. Although afforded the opportunity, he did not take the witness stand. The judge found him guilty and imposed a sentence of eight years.

While serving his sentence, [Betts] filed with a judge of the Circuit Court for Washington County, Maryland, a petition for a writ of habeas corpus [an order to appear before a judge] alleging that he had been deprived of the right to assistance of counsel guaranteed by the Fourteenth Amendment of the Federal Constitution. The . . . [case] was heard, his contention was rejected, and he was remanded [returned] to the custody of the prison warden [Patrick Brady].

Some months later a [second] petition for a writ of habeas corpus was presented to Carroll T. Bond, Chief Judge of the Court of Appeals of Maryland, setting up the same grounds for the prisoner's release as the former petition. . . . [The case] was [again] argued. Judge Bond . . . denied the relief prayed [requested] and remanded [Betts] to [Brady's] custody.

[Betts] applied to [the United States Supreme Court] for certiorari [a judicial review]. . . . [We agreed to hear the case on account of the importance of . . . conflicting decisions upon the constitutional question presented . . . :

> Was [Betts'] conviction and sentence a deprivation of his liberty without due process of law, in violation of the Fourteenth Amendment, because of the court's refusal to appoint counsel at his request?

The Sixth Amendment of the national Constitution applies only to trials in federal courts. The Due Process Clause of the Fourteenth Amendment does not incorporate, as such, the specific guarantees found in the Sixth Amendment although a denial by a state of rights or privileges specifically embodied in that and others of the first eight amendments may, in certain circumstances, or in connection with other elements, operate, in a given case, to deprive a litigant [party to a case] of due process of law in violation of the Fourteenth. Due process of law is secured against invasion by the federal Government by the Fifth Amendment and is safeguarded against state action in identical words by the Fourteenth. The phrase formulates a concept less rigid and more fluid than those envisaged in other specific and particular provisions of the Bill of Rights. Its application is less a matter of rule. Asserted denial is to be tested by an appraisal of the totality of facts in a given case. That which may, in one setting, constitute a denial of fundamental fairness, shocking to the universal sense of justice, may, in other circumstances, and in the light of other considerations, fall short of such denial. In the application of such a concept there is always the danger of falling into the habit of formulating the guarantee into a set of hard and fast rules the application of which in a given case may be to ignore the qualifying factors therein disclosed.

[Betts], in this instance, asks us, in effect, to apply a rule in the enforcement of the Due Process Clause. He says the rule to be deduced from our former decisions is that, in every case, whatever the circumstances, one charged with crime, who is unable to obtain counsel, must be furnished counsel by the state. Expressions in the opinions of this court lend color to the argument, but, as [Betts] admits, none of our decisions squarely adjudicates [determines] the questions now presented.

In *Powell v. Alabama*, ignorant and friendless negro youths, strangers in the community, without friends or means to obtain counsel, were hurried to trial for a capital offense [one in which the death penalty may be imposed] without effective appointment of counsel on whom the burden of preparation and trial would rest, and without adequate opportunity to consult even the counsel casually appointed to represent them. This occurred in a State whose statute law required the appointment of counsel for indigent defendants prosecuted for the offense charged. Thus the trial was conducted in disregard of every principle of fairness and in disregard of that which was declared by the law of the State a requisite of a fair trial. This court held the resulting convictions were without due process of law. It said that, in the light of all the facts, the failure of the trial court to afford the defendants reasonable time and opportunity to secure counsel was a clear denial of due process. The court stated further that "under the circumstances, the necessity of counsel was so vital and imperative that the failure of the trial court to make an effective appointment of counsel was likewise a denial of due process," but added:

> "whether this would be so in other criminal prosecutions, or under other circumstances, we need not determine. All that it is necessary now to decide, as we do decide, is that, in a capital case, where the defendant is unable to employ counsel, and is incapable adequately of making his own defense because of ignorance, feeble-mindedness, illiteracy, or the like, it is the duty of the court, whether requested or not, to assign counsel for him as a necessary requisite of due process of law."

Likewise, in *Avery v. Alabama*, the state law required the appointment of counsel. The claim which we felt required examination, as in the *Powell* Case, was that the purported compliance with this requirement amounted to mere lip service. Scrutiny of the record disclosed that counsel had been appointed and the defendant [party accused of wrongdoing] had been afforded adequate opportunity to prepare his defense with the aid of counsel. We, therefore, overruled the contention that due process had been denied.

In *Smith v. O'Grady* the petition for habeas corpus alleged a failure to appoint counsel but averred other facts which, if established, would prove that the trial was a mere sham and pretense, offensive to the concept of due process. There also, state law required the appointment of counsel for one on trial for the offense involved.

Those cases, which are [Betts'] chief reliance, do not rule this. The question we are now to decide is whether due process of law demands that in every criminal case, whatever the circumstances, a state must furnish counsel to an indigent defendant. Is the furnishing of counsel in all cases whatever dictated by natural, inherent, and fundamental principles of fairness? The answer to the question may be found in the common understanding of those who have lived under the Anglo-American system of law. By the Sixth Amendment the people ordained that, in all criminal prosecutions, the accused should "enjoy the right . . . to have the assistance of counsel for his defense." We have construed [interpreted] the provision to require appointment of counsel in all cases where a defendant is unable to procure the services of an attorney, and where the right has not been intentionally and competently waived. Though, as we have noted, the amendment lays down no rule for the conduct of the states, the question recurs whether the constraint laid by the amendment upon the national courts expresses a rule so fundamental and essential to a fair trial, and so, to due process of law, that it is made obligatory upon the states by the Fourteenth Amendment. Relevant data on the subject are afforded by constitutional and statutory provisions subsisting in the colonies and the states prior to the inclusion of the Bill of Rights in the national Constitution, and in the constitutional, legislative, and judicial history of the states to the present date. These constitute the most authoritative sources for ascertaining the considered judgment of the citizens of the states upon the question.

The Constitutions of the thirteen original states, as they were at the time of federal union, exhibit great diversity in respect of the right to have counsel in criminal cases. Rhode Island had no constitutional provision on the subject until 1843, North Carolina and South Carolina had none until 1868. Virginia has never had any. Maryland, in 1776, and New York, in 1777, adopted provisions to the effect that a defendant accused of crime should be "allowed" counsel. A constitutional mandate that the accused should have a right to be heard by himself and by his counsel was adopted by Pennsylvania in 1776, New Hampshire in 1774, by Delaware in 1782, and by Connecticut in 1818. In 1790 Massachusetts ordained that the defendant should have the right to be heard by himself or his counsel at his election. In 1798 Georgia provided that the accused might be heard by himself or counsel or both. In 1776 New Jersey guaranteed the accused the same privileges of witnesses and counsel as their prosecutors "are or shall be entitled to."

The substance of these provisions of colonial and early state constitutions is explained by the contemporary common law. Originally in England a prisoner was not permitted to be heard by counsel upon the general issue of not guilty on any indictment for treason or felony [a more serious crime]. The practice of English judges, however, was to permit counsel to advise with a defendant as to the conduct of his case and to represent him in collateral matters and as respects questions of law arising upon the trial. In 1695 the rule was relaxed by statute to the extent of permitting one accused of treason the privilege of being heard by counsel. The rule forbidding the participation of counsel stood, however, as to indictments for felony, until 1836, when a statute accorded the right to defend by counsel against summary convictions [before a judge, rather than a jury] and charges of felony. In misdemeanor cases [less serious crimes] and, after 1695, in prosecutions for treason, the rule was that the defense must be conducted either by the defendant in person or by counsel, but that both might not participate in the trial.

In the light of this common law practice, it is evident that the constitutional provisions to the effect that a defendant should be "allowed" counsel or should have a right "to be heard by himself and his counsel," or that he might be heard by "either or both," at his election, were intended to do away with the rules which denied representation, in whole or in part, by counsel in criminal prosecutions, but were not aimed to compel the state to provide counsel for a defendant. At the least, such a construction by state courts and legislators cannot be said to lack reasonable basis.

The statutes in force in the thirteen original states at the time of the adoption of the Bill of Rights are also illuminating. It is of interest that the matter of appointment of counsel for defendants, if dealt with at all, was dealt with by statute rather than by constitutional provision. The contemporary legislation exhibits great diversity of policy.

The Constitutions of all the states, presently in force, save that of Virginia, contain provisions with respect to the assistance of counsel in criminal trials. Those of nine states may be said to embody a guarantee textually the same as that of the Sixth Amendment or of like import. In the fundamental law of most states, however, the language used indicates only that a defendant is not to be denied the privilege of representation by counsel of his choice.

In three states the guarantee, whether or not in the exact phraseology of the Sixth Amendment, has been held to require appointment in all cases where the defendant is unable to procure counsel. In six the provisions (one of which is like the Sixth Amendment) have been held not to require the appointment of counsel for indigent defendants. In eight, provisions, one of which is the same as that of the Sixth Amendment, have evidently not been viewed as requiring such appointment, since the courts have enforced statutes making appointment discretionary, or obligatory only in prosecutions for capital offenses or felonies.

In twelve states it seems to be understood that the constitutional provision does not require appointment of counsel, since statutes of greater or less antiquity call for such appointment only in capital cases or cases of felony or other grave crime, or refer the matter to the discretion of the court. In eighteen states the statutes now require the court to appoint in all cases where defendants are unable to procure counsel. But this has not always been the statutory requirement in some of those states. And it seems to have been assumed by many legislatures that the matter was one for regulation from time to time as deemed necessary, since laws requiring appointment in all cases have been modified to require it only in the case of certain offenses.

This material demonstrates that, in the great majority of the states, it has been the considered judgment of the people, their representatives, and their courts that appointment of counsel is not a fundamental right, essential to a fair trial. On the contrary, the matter has generally been deemed one of legislative policy. In the light of this evidence we are unable to say that the concept of due process incorporated in the Fourteenth Amendment obligates the states, whatever may be their own views, to furnish counsel in every such case. Every court has power, if it deems proper, to appoint counsel where that course seems to be required in the interest of fairness.

The practice of the courts of Maryland gives point to the principle that the states should not be straitjacketed in this respect by a construction of the Fourteenth Amendment. Judge Bond's opinion states . . . that in Maryland the usual practice is for the defendant to waive a trial by jury. This [Betts] did in the present case. Such trials, as Judge Bond remarks, are much more informal than jury trials and it is obvious that the judge can much better control the course of the trial and is in a better position to see impartial justice done than when the formalities of a jury trial are involved.

In this case there was no question of the commission of a robbery. The State's case consisted of evidence identifying [Betts] as the perpetrator. The defense was an alibi. [Betts] called and examined witnesses to prove that he was at another place at the time of the commission of the offense. The simple issue was the veracity of the testimony for the State and that for the defendant. As Judge Bond says, the accused was not helpless, but was a man forty-three years old, of ordinary intelligence and ability to take care of his own interests on the trial of that narrow issue. He had once before been in a criminal court, pleaded guilty to larceny and served a sentence and was not wholly unfamiliar with criminal procedure. It is quite clear that in Maryland, if the situation had been otherwise and it had appeared that [Betts] was, for any reason, at a serious disadvantage by reason of the lack of counsel, a refusal to appoint would have resulted in the reversal of a judgment of conviction. Only recently the [Maryland] Court of Appeals [in *Coates v. State*] has reversed a conviction because it was convinced on the whole record that an accused tried without counsel had been handicapped by the lack of representation.

To deduce from the Due Process Clause a rule binding upon the states in this matter would be to impose upon them, as Judge Bond points out, a requirement without distinction between criminal charges of different magnitude or in respect of courts of varying jurisdiction. As he says:

"Charges of small crimes tried before justices of the peace and capital charges tried in the higher courts would equally require the appointment of counsel. Presumably it would be argued that trials in the Traffic Court would require it."

And indeed it was said by [Betts'] counsel . . . that as the Fourteenth Amendment extends the protection of due process to property as well as to life and liberty, if we hold with [Betts] logic would require the furnishing of counsel in civil cases involving property.

As we have said, the Fourteenth Amendment prohibits the conviction and incarceration of one whose trial is offensive to the common and fundamental ideas of fairness and right, and while want of counsel in a particular case may result in a conviction lacking in such fundamental fairness, we cannot say that the amendment embodies an inexorable command that no trial for any offense, or in any court, can be fairly conducted and justice accorded a defendant who is not represented by counsel. The judgment is affirmed [upheld].

Illegal Search And Seizure
Mapp v. Ohio

The right of the people to be secure in their persons, houses, papers, and effects, against unreasonable searches and seizures, shall not be violated.
- The Fourth Amendment

On May 23, 1957 Cleveland, Ohio police, acting on erroneous information and without having obtained a search warrant, demanded entrance to the home of Dorlee Mapp. She refused police entrance into her home without a search warrant. The police called for back-up and after a three hour standoff broke into the home. Mapp, confronting the police inside her home, again demanded to see a search warrant. A scuffle ensued when the police produced a "warrant" (later found to be phony) which she grabbed and they forcibly took back from her. Police handcuffed Mapp for her "belligerence" and held her in custody while they searched (later described as a ransacking) the entire Mapp home room by room. In the basement, in a trunk, they found "obscene" materials and, pursuant to Ohio law, arrested Mapp for "possession of obscene, lewd and lascivious" materials.

At her trial, Mapp argued that the Federal Exclusionary Rule, based on the Fourth Amendment's Unreasonable Search and Seizure Clause, which covered only *federal* law enforcement officials, should be extended to all *state* law enforcement officials. The Exclusionary Rule stated that any evidence obtained by law enforcement officials as a result of an illegal search and seizure became inadmissible evidence. The trial rejected this argument and Mapp was found guilty. The Ohio Supreme Court upheld her conviction. Dorlee Mapp appealed to the United States Supreme Court.

On June 19, 1961 the 6-3 decision of the United States Supreme Court was announced by Associate Justice Tom Clark.

The *Mapp* Court

Chief Justice Earl Warren
Appointed Chief Justice by President Eisenhower
Served 1953 - 1969

Associate Justice Hugo Black
Appointed by President Franklin Roosevelt
Served 1937 - 1971

Associate Justice Felix Frankfurter
Appointed by President Franklin Roosevelt
Served 1939 - 1962

Associate Justice William Douglas
Appointed by President Franklin Roosevelt
Served 1939 - 1975

Associate Justice Tom Clark
Appointed by President Truman
Served 1949 - 1967

Associate Justice John Marshall Harlan
Appointed by President Eisenhower
Served 1955 - 1971

Associate Justice William Brennan
Appointed by President Eisenhower
Served 1956 - 1990

Associate Justice Charles Whittaker
Appointed by President Eisenhower
Served 1957 - 1962

Associate Justice Potter Stewart
Appointed by President Eisenhower
Served 1958 - 1981

The legal text of *Mapp v. Ohio* can be found in volume 367 of *United States Reports*. Our edited text follows.

MAPP v. OHIO
June 19, 1961

JUSTICE TOM CLARK: Appellant [Dorlee Mapp] stands convicted of knowingly having had in her possession and under her control certain lewd and lascivious books, pictures, and photographs in violation of . . . Ohio's Revised Code. . . . [T]he Supreme Court of Ohio found that her conviction was valid though "based primarily upon the introduction in evidence of lewd and lascivious books and pictures unlawfully seized during an unlawful search of [her] home. . . ."

On May 23, 1957, three Cleveland police officers arrived at [Mapp's] residence in that city pursuant to information that "a person [was] hiding out in the home, who was wanted for questioning in connection with a recent bombing, and that there was a large amount of policy [gambling] paraphernalia being hidden in the home." Miss Mapp and her daughter by a former marriage lived on the top floor of the two-family dwelling. Upon their arrival at that house, the officers knocked on the door and demanded entrance but [Mapp], after telephoning her attorney, refused to admit them without a search warrant. They advised their headquarters of the situation and undertook a surveillance of the house.

The officers again sought entrance some three hours later when four or more additional officers arrived on the scene. When Miss Mapp did not come to the door immediately, at least one of the several doors to the house was forcibly opened and the policemen gained admittance. Meanwhile Miss Mapp's attorney arrived, but the officers, having secured their own entry, and continuing in their defiance of the law, would permit him neither to see Miss Mapp nor to enter the house. It appears that Miss Mapp was halfway down the stairs from the upper floor to the front door when the officers, in this highhanded manner, broke into the hall. She demanded to see the search warrant. A paper, claimed to be a warrant, was held up by one of the officers. She grabbed the "warrant" and placed it in her bosom. A struggle ensued in which the officers recovered the piece of paper and as a result of which they handcuffed [Mapp] because she had been "belligerent" in resisting their official rescue of the "warrant" from her person. Running roughshod over [Mapp], a policeman "grabbed" her, "twisted [her] hand," and she "yelled [and] pleaded with him" because "it was hurting." [Mapp], in handcuffs, was then forcibly taken upstairs to her bedroom where the officers searched a dresser, a chest of drawers, a closet and some suitcases. They also looked into a photo album and through personal papers belonging to [Mapp]. The search spread to the rest of the second floor including the child's bedroom, the living room, the kitchen and a dinette. The basement of the building and a trunk found therein were also searched. The obscene materials for possession of which she was ultimately convicted were discovered in the course of that widespread search.

At the trial, no search warrant was produced by the prosecution, nor was the failure to produce one explained or accounted for. At best, "There is, in the record, considerable doubt as to whether there ever was any warrant for the search of [Mapp]'s home." The Ohio Supreme Court believed a "reasonable argument" could be made that the conviction should be reversed "because the 'methods' employed to obtain the [evidence] . . . were such as to 'offend "a sense of justice,"'" but the court found determinative the fact that the evidence had not been taken "from [Mapp]'s person by the use of brutal or offensive physical force against [her]."

The State says that even if the search were made without authority, or otherwise unreasonably, it is not prevented from using the unconstitutionally seized evidence at trial, citing *Wolf v. Colorado*, in which this Court did indeed hold "that in a prosecution in a State court for a State crime the Fourteenth Amendment does not forbid the admission of evidence obtained by an unreasonable search and seizure."

On this appeal . . . it is urged once again that we review that holding. Seventy-five years ago, in *Boyd v. United States*, considering the Fourth and Fifth Amendments as running "almost into each other" on the facts before it, this Court held that the doctrines of those Amendments "apply to all invasions on the part of the government and its employees of the sanctity of a man's home and the privacies of life. It is not the breaking of his doors, and the rummaging of his drawers, that constitutes the essence of the offense; but it is the invasion of his indefeasible right of personal security, personal liberty and private property. . . . Breaking into a house and opening boxes and drawers are circumstances of aggravation; but any forcible and compulsory extortion of a man's own testimony or of his private papers to be used as evidence to convict him of crime or to forfeit his goods, is within the condemnation . . . [of those Amendments]."

The Court noted that

"constitutional provisions for the security of person and property should be liberally construed. . . . It is the duty of courts to be watchful for the constitutional rights of the citizen, and against any stealthy encroachments thereon."

In this jealous regard for maintaining the integrity of individual rights, the Court gave life to Madison's prediction that "independent tribunals of justice . . . will be naturally led to resist every encroachment upon rights expressly stipulated for in the Constitution by the declaration of rights." Concluding, the Court specifically referred to the use of the evidence there seized as "unconstitutional."

Less than 30 years after *Boyd*, this Court, in *Weeks v. United States*, stated that "the Fourth Amendment . . . put the courts of the United States and Federal officials, in the exercise of their power and authority, under limitations and restraints [and] . . . forever secure[d] the people, their persons, houses, papers and effects against all unreasonable searches and seizures under the guise of law . . . and the duty of giving to it force and effect is obligatory upon all entrusted under our Federal system with the enforcement of the laws."

Specifically dealing with the use of the evidence unconstitutionally seized, the Court concluded: "If letters and private documents can thus be seized and held and used in evidence against a citizen accused of an offense, the protection of the Fourth

Amendment declaring his right to be secure against such searches and seizures is of no value, and, so far as those thus placed are concerned, might as well be stricken from the Constitution. The efforts of the courts and their officials to bring the guilty to punishment, praiseworthy as they are, are not to be aided by the sacrifice of those great principles established by years of endeavor and suffering which have resulted in their embodiment in the fundamental law of the land."

Finally, the Court in that case clearly stated that use of the seized evidence involved "a denial of the constitutional rights of the accused." Thus, in the year 1914, in the *Weeks* case, this Court "for the first time" held that "in a federal prosecution, the Fourth Amendment barred the use of evidence secured through an illegal search and seizure." This Court has ever since required of federal law officers a strict adherence to that command which this Court has held to be a clear, specific, and constitutionally required - even if judicially implied - deterrent safeguard without insistence upon which the Fourth Amendment would have been reduced to "a form of words." It meant, quite simply, that "conviction by means of unlawful seizures and enforced confessions . . . should find no sanction in the judgments of the courts . . . " and that such evidence "shall not be used at all."

. . . . In *Byars v. United States*, a unanimous Court declared that "the doctrine [cannot] . . . be tolerated under our constitutional system, that evidences of crime discovered by a federal officer in making a search without lawful warrant may be used against the victim of the unlawful search where a timely challenge has been interposed." The Court, in *Olmstead v. United States*, in unmistakable language restated the *Weeks* rule, "The striking outcome of the *Weeks* case and those which followed it was the sweeping declaration that the Fourth Amendment, although not referring to or limiting the use of evidence in courts, really forbade its introduction if obtained by government officers through a violation of the Amendment."

In *McNabb v. United States*, we note this statement, "[A] conviction in the federal courts, the foundation of which is evidence obtained in disregard of liberties deemed fundamental by the

Constitution, cannot stand." And this Court has, on Constitutional grounds, set aside convictions, both in the federal and state courts, which were based upon confessions "secured by protracted and repeated questioning of ignorant and untutored persons, in whose minds the power of officers was greatly magnified" . . . or "who have been unlawfully held incommunicado without advice of friends or counsel."

. . . . In 1949, 35 years after *Weeks* was announced, this Court in *Wolf v. Colorado,* again for the first time, discussed the effect of the Fourth Amendment upon the States through the operation of the Due Process Clause of the Fourteenth Amendment. It said, "[W]e have no hesitation in saying that were a State affirmatively to sanction such police incursion into privacy it would run counter to the guaranty of the Fourteenth Amendment."

Nevertheless, after declaring that the "security of one's privacy against arbitrary intrusion by the police" is "implicit in 'the concept of ordered liberty' and as such enforceable against the States through the Due Process Clause," and announcing that it "stoutly adhere[d]" to the *Weeks* decision, the Court decided that the *Weeks* exclusionary rule would not then be imposed upon the States as "an essential ingredient of the right." The Court's reasons for not considering essential to the right to privacy, as a curb imposed upon the States by the Due Process Clause, that which decades before had been posited as part and parcel of the Fourth Amendment's limitation upon federal encroachment of individual privacy, were bottomed on factual considerations.

. . . [W]e will consider the current validity of the factual grounds upon which *Wolf* was based.

The Court in *Wolf* first stated that "[t]he contrariety of views of the States" on the adoption of the exclusionary rule of *Weeks* was "particularly impressive"; and, in this connection, that it could not "brush aside the experience of States which deem the incidence of such conduct by the police too slight to call for a deterrent remedy . . . by overriding the [States'] relevant rules of evidence." While in 1949, prior to the *Wolf* case, almost two-thirds of the States were opposed to the use of the exclusionary rule, now, despite the *Wolf* case, more than half of those since passing upon it, by their own legislative or judicial decision, have wholly or partly adopted or adhered to the *Weeks* rule. Significantly, among those now following the rule is California, which, according to its highest court, was "compelled to reach that conclusion because other remedies have completely failed to secure compliance with the constitutional provisions. . . ." In connection with this California case [*People v. Cahan*], we note that the second basis elaborated in *Wolf* in support of its failure to enforce the exclusionary doctrine against the States was that "other means of protection" have been afforded "the right to privacy." The experience of California that such other remedies have been worthless and futile is buttressed by the experience of other States. The obvious futility of relegating the Fourth Amendment to the protection of other remedies has, moreover, been recognized by this Court since *Wolf*.

Likewise, time has set its face against what *Wolf* called the "weighty testimony" of *People v. Defore*. There, Justice (then Judge) Cardozo, rejecting adoption of the *Weeks* exclusionary rule in New York, had said that "[t]he Federal rule as it stands is either too strict or too lax." However, the force of that reasoning has been largely vitiated by later decisions of this Court. These include the recent discarding of the "silver platter" doctrine which allowed federal judicial use of evidence seized in violation of the Constitution by state agents; the relaxation of the formerly strict requirements as to standing to challenge the use of evidence thus seized, so that now the procedure of exclusion, "ultimately referable to constitutional safeguards," is available to anyone even "legitimately on [the] premises" unlawfully searched; and, finally, the formulation of a method to prevent state use of evidence unconstitutionally seized by federal agents. Because there can be no fixed formula, we are admittedly met with "recurring questions of the reasonableness of searches," but less is not to be expected when dealing with a Constitution, and, at any rate, "[r]easonableness is in the first instance for the [trial court] . . . to determine."

It therefore plainly appears that the factual considerations supporting the failure of the *Wolf* Court to include the *Weeks* exclusionary rule when it recognized the enforceability of the right to privacy against the States in 1949, while not basically relevant to the constitutional consideration, could not, in any analysis, now be deemed controlling.

Some five years after *Wolf*, in answer to a plea made here Term after Term that we overturn its doctrine on applicability of the *Weeks* exclusionary rule, this Court indicated that such should not be done until the States had "adequate opportunity to adopt or reject the [*Weeks*] rule."

. . . . And only last Term, after again carefully reexamining the *Wolf* doctrine in *Elkins v. United States,* the Court pointed out that "the controlling principles" as to search and seizure and the problem of admissibility "seemed clear" until the announcement in *Wolf* "that the Due Process Clause of the Fourteenth Amendment does not itself require state courts to adopt the exclusionary rule" of the *Weeks* case. At the same time, the Court pointed out, "the underlying constitutional doctrine which *Wolf* established . . . that the Federal Constitution . . . prohibits unreasonable searches and seizures by state officers" had undermined the "foundation upon which the admissibility of state-seized evidence in a federal trial originally rested. . . ." The Court concluded that it was therefore obliged to hold . . . that all evidence obtained by an unconstitutional search and seizure was inadmissible in a federal court regardless of its source. Today we once again examine *Wolf*'s constitutional documentation of the right to privacy free from unreasonable state intrusion, and, after its dozen years on our books, are led by it to close the only courtroom door remaining open to evidence secured by official lawlessness in flagrant abuse of that basic right, reserved to all persons as a specific guarantee against that very same unlawful conduct. We hold that all evidence obtained by searches and seizures in violation of the Constitution is, by that same authority, inadmissible in a state court.

Since the Fourth Amendment's right of privacy has been declared enforceable against the States through the Due Process Clause of the Fourteenth, it is enforceable against them by the same sanction of exclusion as is used against the Federal Government. Were it otherwise, then just as without the *Weeks* rule the assurance against unreasonable federal searches and seizures would be "a form of words," . . . so too, without that rule, the freedom from state invasions of privacy would be so ephemeral . . . as not to merit this Court's high regard as a freedom "implicit in the concept of ordered liberty." At the time that the Court held in *Wolf* that the Amendment was applicable to the States through the Due Process Clause, the cases of this Court, as we have seen, had steadfastly held that as to federal officers the Fourth Amendment included the exclusion of the evidence seized in violation of its provisions. Even *Wolf* "stoutly adhered" to that proposition. . . . [I]n extending the substantive [essential] protections of due process to all constitutionally unreasonable searches - state or federal - it was logically and constitutionally necessary that the exclusion doctrine - an essential part of the right to privacy - be also insisted upon as an essential ingredient of the right newly recognized by the *Wolf* case. In short, the admission of the new constitutional right by *Wolf* could not consistently tolerate denial of its most important constitutional privilege, namely, the exclusion of the evidence which an accused had been forced to give by reason of the unlawful seizure. To hold otherwise is to grant the right but in reality to withhold its privilege and enjoyment. Only last year, the Court itself recognized that the purpose of the exclusionary rule "is to deter - to compel respect for the constitutional guaranty in the only effectively available way - by removing the incentive to disregard it."

Indeed, we are aware of no restraint . . . conditioning the enforcement of any other basic constitutional right. The right to privacy, no less important than any other right carefully and particularly reserved to the people, would stand in marked contrast to all other rights declared as "basic to a free society." This Court has not hesitated to enforce as strictly against the States as it does against the Federal Government the rights of free speech and of a free press, the rights to notice and to a fair, public trial, including, as it does, the right not to be convicted by use of a coerced confession, however logically relevant it be, and without regard to its reliability. And nothing could be more certain than that when a coerced confession is involved, "the relevant rules of evidence" are overridden without regard to "the incidence of such conduct by the police," slight or frequent. Why should not the same rule apply to what is tantamount to coerced testimony by way of unconstitutional seizure of goods, papers, effects, documents, etc.? We find that, as to the Federal Government, the Fourth and Fifth Amendments and, as to the States, the freedom from unconscionable invasions of privacy and the freedom from convictions based upon coerced confessions do enjoy an "intimate relation" in their perpetuation of "principles of humanity and civil liberty [secured] . . . only after years of struggle." They express "supplementing phases of the same constitutional purpose - to maintain inviolate large areas of personal privacy." The philosophy of each Amendment and of each freedom is complementary to, although not dependent upon, that of the other in its sphere of influence - the very least that together they assure in either sphere is that no man is to be convicted on unconstitutional evidence.

Moreover, our holding that the exclusionary rule is an essential part of both the Fourth and Fourteenth Amendments is not only the logical dictate of prior cases, but it also makes very good sense. There is no war between the Constitution and common sense. Presently, a federal prosecutor may make no use of evidence illegally seized, but a State's attorney across the street may, although he supposedly is operating under the enforceable prohibitions of the same Amendment. Thus the State, by admitting evidence unlawfully seized, serves to encourage disobedience to the Federal Constitution which it is bound to uphold. . . . Yet the double standard recognized until today hardly put such a thesis into practice. In nonexclusionary States, federal officers, being human, were by it invited to and did . . . step across the street to the State's attorney with their unconstitutionally seized evidence. Prosecution on the basis of that evidence was then had in a state court in utter disregard of the enforceable Fourth Amendment. If the fruits of an unconstitutional search had been inadmissible in both state and federal courts, this inducement to evasion would have been sooner eliminated. . . .

Federal-state cooperation in the solution of crime under constitutional standards will be promoted, if only by recognition of their now mutual obligation to respect the same fundamental criteria in their approaches. . . . Denying shortcuts to only one of two cooperating law enforcement agencies tends naturally to breed legitimate suspicion of "working arrangements" whose results are equally tainted.

There are those who say, as did Justice (then Judge) Cardozo, that under our constitutional exclusionary doctrine "[t]he criminal is to go free because the constable has blundered." In some cases, this will undoubtedly be the result. But, as we said in *Elkins,* "there is another consideration - the imperative of judicial integrity." The criminal goes free, if he must, but it is the law that sets him free. Nothing can destroy a government more quickly than its failure to observe its own laws, or worse, its disregard of the charter of its own existence. As Justice Brandeis, dissenting, said in *Olmstead:*

> "Our Government is the potent, the omnipresent teacher. For good or for ill, it teaches the whole people by its example. . . . If the Government becomes a lawbreaker, it breeds contempt for law; it invites every man to become a law unto himself; it invites anarchy."

Nor can it lightly be assumed that, as a practical matter, adoption of the exclusionary rule fetters law enforcement. Only last year, this Court expressly considered that contention and found that "pragmatic evidence of a sort" to the contrary was not wanting. The Court noted that, "The federal courts themselves have operated under the exclusionary rule of *Weeks* for almost half a century; yet it has not been suggested either that the Federal Bureau of Investigation has thereby been rendered ineffective, or that the administration of criminal justice in the federal courts has thereby been disrupted. Moreover, the experience of the states is impressive. . . . The movement towards the rule of exclusion has been halting, but seemingly inexorable."

The ignoble shortcut to conviction left open to the State tends to destroy the entire system of constitutional restraints on which the liberties of the people rest. Having once recognized that the right to privacy embodied in the Fourth Amendment is enforceable against the States, and that the right to be secure against rude invasions of privacy by state officers is, therefore, constitutional in origin, we can no longer permit that right to remain an empty promise. Because it is enforceable in the same manner and to like effect as other basic rights secured by the Due Process Clause, we can no longer permit it to be revocable at the whim of any police officer who, in the name of law enforcement itself, chooses to suspend its enjoyment. Our decision, founded on reason and truth, gives to the individual no more than that which the Constitution guarantees him, to the police officer no less than that to which honest law enforcement is entitled, and, to the courts, that judicial integrity so necessary in the administration of justice.

The judgment of the Supreme Court of Ohio is reversed and the [case] remanded [returned to the lower court] for further proceedings not inconsistent with this opinion.

Indigent Defendants
Gideon v. Wainwright

I, Clarence Earl Gideon, claim that I was denied the rights of the Fourth, Fifth, and Fourteenth Amendments of the Bill of Rights.
- The Gideon Petition

In June 1961 Clarence Earl Gideon was arrested in Bay Harbor, Florida on a felony charge of breaking and entering. Gideon asked the Florida Circuit Court, in which he was to be tried, to appoint a lawyer to defend him. The Court answered: *Mr. Gideon, I am sorry, but I cannot appoint counsel to represent you in this case. Under the laws of the State of Florida, the only time the Court can appoint counsel to represent a defendant is when that person is charged with a capital offense. I am sorry, but I will have to deny your request to appoint counsel to defend you in this case.* Gideon pled not guilty and defended himself as best he could. A jury found him guilty and he was sentenced to five years in a Florida State Prison.

Gideon appealed his conviction and sentence to the Florida Supreme Court, claiming that the trial judge's refusal to appoint a defense lawyer to represent him was a denial of rights "guaranteed by the Constitution and the Bill of Rights." The Florida Supreme Court denied his appeal.

Gideon, in a handwritten petition, appealed to the U.S. Supreme Court to overturn his conviction and sentence. The Court agreed to hear his case and appointed a lawyer to represent him. In 1942 the Court had held in the *Betts v. Brady* decision that the Sixth Amendment's "Right To The Assistance Of Counsel Clause" did not extend to criminal defendants in state cases. Gideon allowed the Court to reconsider.

On March 18, 1963 the 9-0 decision of the U.S. Supreme Court was announced by Associate Justice Hugo Black.

The *Gideon* Court

Chief Justice Earl Warren
Appointed Chief Justice by President Eisenhower
Served 1953 - 1969

Associate Justice Hugo Black
Appointed by President Franklin Roosevelt
Served 1937 - 1971

Associate Justice William Douglas
Appointed by President Franklin Roosevelt
Served 1939 - 1975

Associate Justice Tom Clark
Appointed by President Truman
Served 1949 - 1967

Associate Justice John Marshall Harlan
Appointed by President Eisenhower
Served 1955 - 1971

Associate Justice William Brennan
Appointed by President Eisenhower
Served 1956 - 1990

Associate Justice Potter Stewart
Appointed by President Eisenhower
Served 1958 - 1981

Associate Justice Byron White
Appointed by President Kennedy
Served 1962 - 1993

Associate Justice Arthur Goldberg
Appointed by President Kennedy
Served 1962 - 1965

The legal text of *Gideon v. Wainwright* can be found in volume 372 of *United States Reports*. Our edited text follows.

GIDEON *v.* WAINWRIGHT
March 18, 1963

JUSTICE HUGO BLACK: Petitioner [Clarence Gideon] was charged in a Florida state court with having broken and entered a poolroom with intent to commit a misdemeanor [crime lower than a felony]. This offense is a felony under Florida law. Appearing in court without funds and without a lawyer, [Gideon] asked the court to appoint counsel for him, whereupon the following colloquy took place:

> "The Court: Mr. Gideon, I am sorry, but I cannot appoint Counsel to represent you in this case. Under the laws of the State of Florida, the only time the Court can appoint Counsel to represent a Defendant is when that person is charged with a capital offense [one carrying a possible death penalty]. I am sorry, but I will have to deny your request to appoint Counsel to defend you in this case.

> "The Defendant: The United States Supreme Court says I am entitled to be represented by Counsel."

Put to trial before a jury, Gideon conducted his defense about as well as could be expected from a layman. He made an opening statement to the jury, cross-examined the State's witnesses, presented witnesses in his own defense, declined to testify himself, and made a short argument "emphasizing his innocence to the charge contained in the Information filed in this case." The jury returned a verdict of guilty, and [Gideon] was sentenced to serve five years in the state prison. Later, [he] filed in the Florida Supreme Court this habeas corpus petition [questioning the legality of his imprisonment, against Wainwright, the Director of Corrections] attacking his conviction and sentence on the ground that the trial court's refusal to appoint counsel for him denied him rights "guaranteed by the Constitution and the Bill of Rights by the United States Government." . . . [T]he State Supreme Court [refused his petition]. Since 1942, when *Betts v. Brady* was decided by a divided [U.S. Supreme] Court, the problem of a defendant's federal constitutional right to counsel in a state court has been a continuing source of controversy and litigation in both state and federal courts. To give this problem another review here, we granted certiorari [agreed to hear the case]. Since Gideon was proceeding in forma pauperis [without funds], we appointed counsel to represent him and requested both sides to discuss in their briefs and oral arguments the following: "Should this Court's holding in *Betts v. Brady* be reconsidered?"

The facts upon which Betts claimed that he had been unconstitutionally denied the right to have counsel appointed to assist him are strikingly like the facts upon which Gideon here bases his federal constitutional claim. Betts was indicted for robbery in a Maryland state court. On arraignment [appearance before the court to enter a plea of guilt or innocence], he told the trial judge of his lack of funds to hire a lawyer and asked the court to appoint one for him. Betts was advised that it was not the practice in that county to appoint counsel for indigent defendants except in murder and rape cases. He then pleaded not guilty, had witnesses summoned, cross-examined the State's witnesses, examined his own, and chose not to testify himself. He was found guilty by the judge, sitting without a jury, and sentenced to eight years in prison. Like Gideon, Betts sought release by habeas corpus, alleging that he had been denied the right to assistance of counsel in violation of the Fourteenth Amendment. Betts was denied any relief and on review this Court affirmed [let the lower court ruling stand]. It was held that a refusal to appoint counsel for an indigent defendant charged with a felony did not necessarily violate the Due Process Clause of the Fourteenth Amendment, which for reasons given the Court deemed to be the only applicable federal constitutional provision. The Court said:

> "Asserted denial [of due process] is to be tested by an appraisal of the totality of facts in a given case. That which may, in one setting, constitute a denial of fundamental fairness, shocking to the universal sense of justice, may, in other circumstances, and in the light of other considerations, fall short of such denial."

Treating due process as "a concept less rigid and more fluid than those envisaged in other specific and particular provisions of the

Bill of Rights," the Court held that refusal to appoint counsel under the particular facts and circumstances in the *Betts* case was not so "offensive to the common and fundamental ideas of fairness" as to amount to a denial of due process. Since the facts and circumstances of the two cases are so nearly indistinguishable, we think the *Betts v. Brady* holding if left standing would require us to reject Gideon's claim that the Constitution guarantees him the assistance of counsel. Upon full reconsideration we conclude that *Betts v. Brady* should be overruled.

The Sixth Amendment provides, "In all criminal prosecutions, the accused shall enjoy the right . . . to have the Assistance of Counsel for his defense." We have construed [interpreted] this to mean that in federal courts counsel must be provided for defendants unable to employ counsel unless the right is competently and intelligently waived. Betts argued that this right is extended to indigent defendants in state courts by the Fourteenth Amendment. In response the Court stated that, while the Sixth Amendment laid down "no rule for the conduct of the States, the question recurs whether the constraint laid by the Amendment upon the national courts expresses a rule so fundamental and essential to a fair trial, and so, to due process of law, that it is made obligatory upon the States by the Fourteenth Amendment." In order to decide whether the Sixth Amendment's guarantee of counsel is of this fundamental nature, the Court in *Betts* set out and considered "[r]elevant data on the subject . . . afforded by constitutional and statutory provisions subsisting in the colonies and the States prior to the inclusion of the Bill of Rights in the national Constitution, and in the constitutional, legislative, and judicial history of the States to the present date." On the basis of this historical data, the Court concluded that "appointment of counsel is not a fundamental right, essential to a fair trial." It was for this reason the *Betts* Court refused to accept the contention that the Sixth Amendment's guarantee of counsel for indigent federal defendants was extended to or, in the words of that Court, "made obligatory upon, the States by the Fourteenth Amendment." Plainly, had the Court concluded that appointment of counsel for an indigent criminal defendant was "a fundamental right, essential to a fair trial," it would have held that the Fourteenth Amendment requires appointment of counsel in a state court, just as the Sixth Amendment requires in a federal court. We think the Court in *Betts* had ample precedent for acknowledging that those guarantees of the Bill of Rights which are fundamental safeguards of liberty immune from federal abridgment are equally protected against state invasion by the Due Process Clause of the Fourteenth Amendment. . . . [I]n *Powell v. Alabama* . . . the Court held that . . . the Fourteenth Amendment "embraced" those "fundamental principles of liberty and justice which lie at the base of all our civil and political institutions," even though they had been "specifically dealt with in another part of the federal Constitution." In many cases other than *Powell* and *Betts*, this Court has looked to the fundamental nature of original Bill of Rights guarantees to decide whether the Fourteenth Amendment makes them obligatory on the States. Explicitly recognized to be of this "fundamental nature" and therefore made immune from state invasion by the Fourteenth, or some part of it, are the First Amendment's freedoms of speech, press, religion, assembly, association, and petition for redress of grievances. For the same reason . . . the Court has made obligatory on the States the Fifth Amendment's command that private property shall not be taken for public use without just compensation, the Fourth Amendment's prohibition of unreasonable searches and seizures, and the Eighth's ban on cruel and unusual punishment. On the other hand, this Court in *Palko v. Connecticut* refused to hold that the Fourteenth Amendment made the double jeopardy provision of the Fifth Amendment obligatory on the States. In so refusing, however, the Court, speaking through Justice Cardozo, was careful to emphasize that "immunities that are valid as against the federal government by force of the specific pledges of particular amendments have been found to be implicit in the concept of ordered liberty, and thus, through the Fourteenth Amendment, become valid as against the states." . . .

We accept *Betts'* assumption, based as it was on our prior cases, that a provision of the Bill of Rights which is "fundamental and essential to a fair trial" is made obligatory upon the States by the Fourteenth Amendment. We think the Court in *Betts* was wrong, however, in concluding that the Sixth Amendment's guarantee of counsel is not one of these fundamental rights. Ten years before *Betts*, this Court . . . had unequivocally declared that "the right to the aid of counsel is of this fundamental character." While the Court . . . [limited] its holding to the particular facts and circumstances of that case, its conclusions about the fundamental nature of the right to counsel are unmistakable. Several years later, in 1936 [in *Grosjean v. American Press*], the Court reemphasized what it had said about the fundamental nature of the right to counsel in this language: "We concluded that certain fundamental rights, safeguarded by the first eight amendments against federal action, were also safeguarded against state action by the due process of law clause of the Fourteenth Amendment, and among them the fundamental right of the accused to the aid of counsel in a criminal prosecution."

And again in 1938 [in *Johnson v. Zerbst*], this Court said:

"[The assistance of counsel] is one of the safeguards of the Sixth Amendment deemed necessary to insure fundamental human rights of life and liberty. . . . The Sixth Amendment stands as a constant admonition that if the constitutional safeguards it provides be lost, justice will not 'still be done.'"

In light of these and many other prior decisions of this Court, it is not surprising that the *Betts* Court, when faced with the contention that "one charged with crime, who is unable to obtain counsel, must be furnished counsel by the State," conceded that "[e]xpressions in the opinions of this court lend color to the argument. . . ." The fact is that in deciding as it did - that "appointment of counsel is not a fundamental right, essential to a fair trial" - the Court in *Betts* made an abrupt break with its own well-considered precedents. In returning to these old precedents, sounder we believe than the new, we but restore constitutional principles established to achieve a fair system of justice. Not only these precedents but also reason and reflection require us to recognize that in our adversary system of criminal justice, any person hauled into court, who is too poor to hire a lawyer, cannot be assured a fair trial unless counsel is provided for him. This seems to us to be an obvious truth. Governments, both state and federal, quite properly spend vast sums of money to establish machinery to try defendants accused of crime. Lawyers to prosecute are everywhere deemed essential to protect the public's interest in an orderly society. Similarly, there are few defendants charged with crime, few indeed, who fail to hire the best lawyers they can get to prepare and present their defenses. That government hires lawyers to prosecute and defendants who have the money hire lawyers to defend are the strongest indications of the widespread belief that lawyers in criminal courts are necessities, not luxuries. The right of one charged with crime to counsel may not be deemed fundamental and essential to fair trials in some countries, but it is in ours. From the very beginning, our state and national constitutions and laws have laid great emphasis on procedural and substantive safeguards designed to assure fair trials before impartial tribunals in which every defendant stands equal before the law. This noble ideal cannot be realized if the poor man charged with crime has to face his accusers without a lawyer to assist him. A defendant's need for a lawyer is nowhere better stated than in the moving words of Justice Sutherland in *Powell v. Alabama*:

"The right to be heard would be, in many cases, of little avail if it did not comprehend the right to be heard by counsel. Even the intelligent and educated layman has small and sometimes no skill in the science of law. If charged with crime, he is incapable, generally, of determining for himself whether the indictment is good or bad. He is unfamiliar with the rules of evidence. Left without the aid of counsel he may be put on trial without a proper charge, and convicted upon incompetent evidence, or evidence irrelevant to the issue or otherwise inadmissible. He lacks both the skill and knowledge adequately to prepare his defense, even though he have a perfect one. He requires the guiding hand of counsel at every step in the proceedings against him. Without it, though he be not guilty, he faces the danger of conviction because he does not know how to establish his innocence."

The Court in *Betts* departed from the sound wisdom upon which the Court's holding in *Powell* rested. Florida, supported by two other States, has asked that *Betts* be left intact. Twenty-two States, as friends of the Court, argue that *Betts* was "an anachronism when handed down" and that it should now be overruled. We agree.

The judgment is reversed, and the cause is remanded [returned] to the Supreme Court of Florida for further action not inconsistent with this opinion.

The Right To Counsel
Escobedo v. Illinois

In all criminal prosecutions the accused shall enjoy the right to have the assistance of counsel for his defense.   **- The Sixth Amendment**

Beginning on the night of January 30 and continuing into the early morning hours of February 1, 1961, Danny Escobedo, twenty-two, was interrogated by the Chicago Police in connection with an unsolved murder. Inside the interrogation room, Escobedo repeatedly asked to be allowed to talk to his lawyer. The police refused and told him, "Your lawyer does not want to talk to you." Outside the interrogation room, Escobedo's lawyer repeatedly demanded that the police allow him to see his client. The police refused and told him, "You cannot talk to your client."

Danny Escobedo, after hours of physical duress (handcuffed and left standing throughout the night) and mentally coercive questioning ("good cop promises - bad cop threats"), made a series of self-incriminating statements. On the basis of these statements obtained by the police during their interrogation and used by the State at his trial, Escobedo was tried and convicted of murder.

On appeal, the Illinois Supreme Court refused to overturn the guilty verdict. Escobedo then appealed to the United States Supreme Court, arguing that the police, in refusing him his right to talk to his lawyer and his lawyer the right to talk to him, had violated his Sixth Amendment right to the assistance of counsel and that no self-incriminating statement extracted by the police during an unconstitutional interrogation could be used against him at a trial.

On June 22, 1964 the 5-4 decision of the United States Supreme Court was announced by Associate Justice Arthur Goldberg.

The *Escobedo* Court

Chief Justice Earl Warren
Appointed Chief Justice by President Eisenhower
Served 1953 - 1969

Associate Justice Hugo Black
Appointed by President Franklin Roosevelt
Served 1937 - 1971

Associate Justice William Douglas
Appointed by President Franklin Roosevelt
Served 1939 - 1975

Associate Justice Tom Clark
Appointed by President Truman
Served 1949 - 1967

Associate Justice John Marshall Harlan
Appointed by President Eisenhower
Served 1955 - 1971

Associate Justice William Brennan
Appointed by President Eisenhower
Served 1956 - 1990

Associate Justice Potter Stewart
Appointed by President Eisenhower
Served 1958 - 1981

Associate Justice Byron White
Appointed by President Kennedy
Served 1962 - 1993

Associate Justice Arthur Goldberg
Appointed by President Kennedy
Served 1962 - 1965

The legal text of *Escobedo v. Illinois* can be found in volume 378 of *United States Reports*. Our edited text follows.

ESCOBEDO v. ILLINOIS
June 22, 1964

JUSTICE ARTHUR GOLDBERG: The critical question in this case is whether, under the circumstances, the refusal by the police to honor petitioner [Danny Escobedo]'s request to consult with his lawyer during the course of an interrogation constitutes a denial of "the Assistance of Counsel" in violation of the Sixth Amendment to the Constitution as "made obligatory upon the States by the Fourteenth Amendment," and thereby renders inadmissible in a state criminal trial any incriminating statement elicited by the police during the interrogation.

On the night of January 19, 1960, [Danny Escobedo]'s brother-in-law was fatally shot. In the early hours of the next morning, at 2:30 a.m., [Escobedo] was arrested without a warrant [a written order] and interrogated. [He] made no statement to the police and was released at 5 that afternoon pursuant to a state court writ of habeas corpus [an order to bring someone to court] obtained by Warren Wolfson, a lawyer who had been retained by [Escobedo].

On January 30, Benedict DiGerlando, who was then in police custody and who was later indicted [charged] for the murder along with [Escobedo], told the police that [Escobedo] had fired the fatal shots. Between 8 and 9 that evening, [Escobedo] and his sister, the widow of the deceased, were arrested and taken to police headquarters. En route to the police station, the police "had handcuffed [him] behind his back," and "one of the arresting officers told [Escobedo] that DiGerlando had named him as the one who shot" the deceased. [Escobedo] testified, without contradiction, that the "detectives said they had us pretty well, up pretty tight, and we might as well admit to this crime," and that he replied, "I am sorry but I would like to have advice from my lawyer." A police officer testified that, although [Escobedo] was not formally charged, "he was in custody" and "couldn't walk out the door."

Shortly after [Escobedo] reached police headquarters, his retained lawyer arrived. The lawyer described the ensuing events in the following terms:

"On that day, I received a phone call [from 'the mother of another defendant'] and pursuant to that phone call, I went to the Detective Bureau at 11th and State. The first person I talked to was the Sergeant on duty at the Bureau Desk, Sergeant Pidgeon. I asked Sergeant Pidgeon for permission to speak to my client, Danny Escobedo. . . . Sergeant Pidgeon made a call to the Bureau lockup and informed me that the boy had been taken from the lockup to the Homicide Bureau. This was between 9:30 and 10:00 in the evening. Before I went anywhere, he called the Homicide Bureau and told them there was an attorney waiting to see Escobedo. He told me I could not see him. Then I went upstairs to the Homicide Bureau. There were several Homicide detectives around, and I talked to them. I identified myself as Escobedo's attorney and asked permission to see him. They said I could not. . . . The police officer told me to see Chief Flynn, who was on duty. I identified myself to Chief Flynn and asked permission to see my client. He said I could not. . . . I think it was approximately 11:00 o'clock. He said I couldn't see him because they hadn't completed questioning. . . . [F]or a second or two, I spotted him in an office in the Homicide Bureau. The door was open, and I could see through the office. . . . I waved to him and he waved back, and then the door was closed by one of the officers at Homicide. There were four or five officers milling around the   Homicide Detail that night.   As to whether I talked to Captain Flynn any later that day, I waited around for another hour or two and went back again and renewed [my] request to see my client. He again told me I could not. . . . I filed an official complaint with Commissioner Phelan of the Chicago Police Department. I had a conversation with every police officer I could find. I was told at Homicide that I couldn't see him and I would have to get a writ of habeas corpus. I left the Homicide Bureau and from the Detective Bureau at 11th and State at approximately 1:00 a.m. [Sunday morning]. I had no opportunity to talk to my client that night. I quoted to Captain Flynn the Section of the

Criminal Code which allows an attorney the right to see his client."

[Danny Escobedo] testified that during the course of the interrogation he repeatedly asked to speak to his lawyer and that the police said that his lawyer "didn't want to see" him. The testimony of the police officers confirmed these accounts in substantial detail.

Notwithstanding repeated requests by each, [Escobedo] and his retained lawyer were afforded no opportunity to consult during the course of the entire interrogation. At one point, as previously noted, [Escobedo] and his attorney came into each other's view for a few moments, but the attorney was quickly ushered away. [Escobedo] testified "that he heard a detective telling the attorney the latter would not be allowed to talk to [him] 'until they were done,'" and that he heard the attorney being refused permission to remain in the adjoining room. A police officer testified that he had told the lawyer that he could not see [Escobedo] until "we were through interrogating" him.

There is testimony by the police that during the interrogation, [Escobedo], a 22-year-old of Mexican extraction with no record of previous experience with the police, "was handcuffed" in a standing position and that he "was nervous, he had circles under his eyes, and he was upset" and was "agitated" because "he had not slept well in over a week."

It is undisputed that during the course of the interrogation Officer Montejano, who "grew up" in [Escobedo's] neighborhood, who knew his family, and who uses "Spanish language in [his] police work," conferred alone with [Escobedo] "for about a quarter of an hour. . . ." [Escobedo] testified that the officer said to him "in Spanish that my sister and I could go home if I pinned it on Benedict DiGerlando," that "he would see to it that we would go home and be held only as witnesses, if anything, if we had made a statement against DiGerlando . . . , that we would be able to go home that night." [Escobedo] testified that he made the statement in issue because of this assurance. Officer Montejano denied offering any such assurance.

A police officer testified that during the interrogation the following occurred:

> "I informed him of what DiGerlando told me and, when I did, he told me that DiGerlando was [lying], and I said, 'Would you care to tell DiGerlando that?' and he said, 'Yes, I will.' So I brought . . . Escobedo in and he confronted DiGerlando and he told him that he was lying and said, 'I didn't shoot Manuel, you did it.'"

In this way, [Escobedo,] for the first time, admitted to some knowledge of the crime. After that, he made additional statements further implicating himself in the murder plot. At this point, an Assistant State's Attorney, Theodore J. Cooper, was summoned "to take" a statement. Mr. Cooper, an experienced lawyer who was assigned to the Homicide Division to take "statements from some defendants and some prisoners that they had in custody," "took" [Escobedo's] statement by asking carefully framed questions apparently designed to assure the admissibility into evidence of the resulting answers. Mr. Cooper testified that he did not advise [Escobedo] of his constitutional rights, and it is undisputed that no one during the course of the interrogation so advised him.

[Danny Escobedo] moved both before and during trial to suppress the incriminating statement, but the motions were denied. [He] was convicted of murder and he appealed the conviction.

The Supreme Court of Illinois, in its original opinion of February 1, 1963, held the statement inadmissible and reversed the conviction. The court said, "[I]t seems manifest to us, from the undisputed evidence and the circumstances surrounding [Escobedo] at the time of his statement and shortly prior thereto, that [he] understood he would be permitted to go home if he gave the statement and would be granted an immunity from prosecution."

The State petitioned for, and the court granted, rehearing. The court then affirmed [upheld] the conviction. It said,

"[T]he officer denied making the promise and the trier of fact [judge or jury] believed him. We find no reason for disturbing the trial court's finding that the confession was voluntary."

The court also held . . . that the confession was admissible even though "it was obtained after he had requested the assistance of counsel, which request was denied." We granted a writ of certiorari [agreed to hear the case] to consider whether [Escobedo's] statement was constitutionally admissible at his trial. We conclude . . . that it was not and, accordingly, we reverse the judgment of conviction.

In *Massiah v. United States*, this Court observed that,

"[A] Constitution which guarantees a defendant the aid of counsel at . . . trial could surely vouchsafe no less to an indicted defendant under interrogation by the police in a completely extrajudicial proceeding. Anything less . . . might deny a defendant 'effective representation by counsel at the only stage when legal aid and advice would help him.'"

The interrogation here was conducted before [Escobedo] was formally indicted. But in the context of this case, that fact should make no difference. When [Escobedo] requested, and was denied, an opportunity to consult with his lawyer, the investigation had ceased to be a general investigation of "an unsolved crime." [Escobedo] had become the accused, and the purpose of the interrogation was to "get him" to confess his guilt despite his constitutional right not to do so. At the time of his arrest and throughout the course of the interrogation, the police told [Escobedo] that they had convincing evidence that he had fired the fatal shots. Without informing him of his absolute right to remain silent in the face of this accusation, the police urged him to make a statement. As this Court observed many years ago, "It cannot be doubted that, placed in the position in which the accused was when the statement was made to him that the other suspected person had charged him with crime, the result was to produce upon his mind the fear that if he remained silent, it would be considered an admission of guilt, and therefore render certain his being committed for trial as the guilty person, and it cannot be conceived that the converse impression would not also have naturally arisen, that, by denying there was hope of removing the suspicion from himself."

[Danny Escobedo], a layman, was undoubtedly unaware that under Illinois law an admission of "mere" complicity in the murder plot was legally as damaging as an admission of firing of the fatal shots. The "guiding hand of counsel" was essential to advise [Escobedo] of his rights in this delicate situation. This was the "stage when legal aid and advice" were most critical to [him]. . . . What happened at this interrogation could certainly "affect the whole trial," since rights "may be as irretrievably lost, if not then and there asserted, as they are when an accused represented by counsel waives a right for strategic purposes." It would exalt form over substance to make the right to counsel, under these circumstances, depend on whether at the time of the interrogation, the authorities had secured a formal indictment. [Escobedo] had, for all practical purposes, already been charged with murder.

The New York Court of Appeals, whose decisions this Court cited with approval in *Massiah,* has recently recognized that, under circumstances such as those here, no meaningful distinction can be drawn between interrogation of an accused before and after formal indictment. In *People v. Donovan,* that court, in an opinion by Judge Fuld, held that "a confession taken from a defendant, during a period of detention [prior to indictment], after his attorney had requested and been denied access to him" could not be used against him in a criminal trial. The court observed that it "would be highly incongruous if our system of justice permitted the district attorney, the lawyer representing the State, to extract a confession from the accused while his own lawyer, seeking to speak with him, was kept from him by the police."

In *Gideon v. Wainwright,* we held that every person accused of a crime, whether state or federal, is entitled to a lawyer at trial. The rule sought by the State here, however, would make the trial no more than an appeal from the interrogation, and the "right to use counsel at the formal trial [would be] a very hollow thing [if], for all practical purposes, the conviction is already assured by pretrial examination." "One can imagine a cynical prosecutor saying, 'Let them have the most illustrious counsel now. They can't escape the noose. There is nothing that counsel can do for them at the trial.'"

It is argued that, if the right to counsel is afforded prior to indictment, the number of confessions obtained by the police will diminish significantly, because most confessions are obtained during the period between arrest and indictment, and "any lawyer worth his salt will tell the suspect in no uncertain terms to make no statement to police under any circumstances." This argument, of course, cuts two ways. The fact that many confessions are obtained during this period points up its critical nature as a "stage when legal aid and advice" are surely needed. The right to counsel would indeed be hollow if it began at a period when few confessions were obtained. There is necessarily a direct relationship between the importance of a stage to the police in their quest for a confession and the criticalness of that stage to the accused in his need for legal advice. Our Constitution, unlike some others, strikes the balance in favor of the right of the accused to be advised by his lawyer of his privilege against self-incrimination.

We have learned the lesson of history, ancient and modern, that a system of criminal law enforcement which comes to depend on the "confession" will, in the long run, be less reliable and more subject to abuses than a system which depends on extrinsic evidence independently secured through skillful investigation. As Dean Wigmore so wisely said,

> "[A]ny system of administration which permits the prosecution to trust habitually to compulsory self-disclosure as a source of proof must itself suffer morally thereby. The inclination develops to rely mainly upon such evidence, and to be satisfied with an incomplete investigation of the other sources. The exercise of the power to extract answers begets a forgetfulness of the just limitations of that power. The simple and peaceful process of questioning breeds a readiness to resort to bullying and to physical force and torture. If there is a right to an answer, there soon seems to be a right to the expected answer - that is, to a confession of guilt. Thus, the legitimate use grows into the unjust abuse; ultimately, the inno-

cent are jeopardized by the encroachments of a bad system. Such seems to have been the course of experience in those legal systems where the privilege was not recognized."

This Court also has recognized that "history amply shows that confessions have often been extorted to save law enforcement officials the trouble and effort of obtaining valid and independent evidence. . . ."

We have also learned the companion lesson of history that no system of criminal justice can, or should, survive if it comes to depend for its continued effectiveness on the citizens' abdication through unawareness of their constitutional rights. No system worth preserving should have to fear that if an accused is permitted to consult with a lawyer, he will become aware of, and exercise, these rights. If the exercise of constitutional rights will thwart the effectiveness of a system of law enforcement, then there is something very wrong with that system.

We hold, therefore, that where, as here, the investigation is no longer a general inquiry into an unsolved crime, but has begun to focus on a particular suspect, the suspect has been taken into police custody, the police carry out a process of interrogations that lends itself to eliciting incriminating statements, the suspect has requested and been denied an opportunity to consult with his lawyer, and the police have not effectively warned him of his absolute constitutional right to remain silent, the accused has been denied "the Assistance of Counsel" in violation of the Sixth Amendment to the Constitution as "made obligatory upon the States by the Fourteenth Amendment," and that no statement elicited by the police during the interrogation may be used against him at a criminal trial.

. . . . Nothing we have said today affects the powers of the police to investigate "an unsolved crime," by gathering information from witnesses and by other "proper investigative efforts." We hold only that when the process shifts from investigatory to accusatory - when its focus is on the accused and its purpose is to elicit a confession - our adversary system begins to operate, and, under the circumstances here, the accused must be permitted to consult with his lawyer.

The judgment of the Illinois Supreme Court is reversed and the case remanded [returned] for proceedings not inconsistent with this opinion.

The Right To Confront Your Accuser
Pointer v. Texas

In all criminal prosecutions, the accused shall enjoy the right to be confronted by witnesses against him.   **- The Sixth Amendment**

On June 16, 1962 Kenneth Phillips, manager of a Houston, Texas 7-11 Food Store was robbed at gunpoint of $375. Bob Pointer, found by police in the neighborhood, was arrested for the crime.

On June 25, 1962, in Harris County's Justice Court, a probable cause hearing (called an examining trial in Texas) was held to determine whether Pointer should be held over for trial. Pointer pled not guilty and offered an unsubstantiated alibi. Philips positively testified that Pointer was the man who had robbed him. On the basis of Philips' testimony, Pointer was ordered to stand trial for armed robbery.

Prior to the beginning of Pointer's trial in Harris County's Criminal District Court, Kenneth Phillips, the State's only witness against Pointer, moved out of Texas. At the trial, prosecutors offered the transcript of Philips' testimony against Pointer given during the examining trial. Pointer objected that this substitution was a direct violation of his Sixth Amendment right to confront the witnesses against him and his Fourteenth Amendment right to due process. Pointer's objections were overruled. The transcript was entered into evidence and, based on the transcript, Pointer was convicted of armed robbery and sentenced to life imprisonment. The Texas Court of Criminal Appeals, finding no error had been committed, upheld his life sentence. Pointer appealed for a final determination to the United States Supreme Court.

On April 5, 1965 the 9-0 decision of the U.S. Supreme Court was announced by Associate Justice Hugo Black.

The *Pointer* Court

Chief Justice Earl Warren
Appointed Chief Justice by President Eisenhower
Served 1953 - 1969

Associate Justice Hugo Black
Appointed by President Franklin Roosevelt
Served 1937 - 1971

Associate Justice William Douglas
Appointed by President Franklin Roosevelt
Served 1939 - 1975

Associate Justice Tom Clark
Appointed by President Truman
Served 1949 - 1967

Associate Justice John Marshall Harlan
Appointed by President Eisenhower
Served 1955 - 1971

Associate Justice William Brennan
Appointed by President Eisenhower
Served 1956 - 1990

Associate Justice Potter Stewart
Appointed by President Eisenhower
Served 1958 - 1981

Associate Justice Byron White
Appointed by President Kennedy
Served 1962 - 1993

Associate Justice Arthur Goldberg
Appointed by President Kennedy
Served 1962 - 1965

The legal text of *Pointer v. Texas* can be found in volume 380 of *United States Reports*. Our edited text follows.

POINTER v. TEXAS
April 5, 1965

JUSTICE HUGO BLACK: The Sixth Amendment provides in part that, "In all criminal prosecutions, the accused shall enjoy the right . . . to be confronted with the witnesses against him . . . and to have the Assistance of Counsel for his defense."

Two years ago, in *Gideon v. Wainwright,* we held that the Fourteenth Amendment makes the Sixth Amendment's guarantee of right to counsel obligatory upon the States. The question we find necessary to decide in this case is whether the Amendment's guarantee of a defendant's right "to be confronted with the witnesses against him," which has been held to include the right to cross-examine those witnesses, is also made applicable to the States by the Fourteenth Amendment.

The petitioner [Bob Granville Pointer] and one Dillard were arrested in Texas and taken before a state judge for a preliminary hearing (in Texas called the "examining trial") on a charge of having robbed Kenneth W. Phillips of $375 "by assault, or violence, or by putting in fear of life or bodily injury." . . . At this hearing, an Assistant District Attorney conducted the prosecution and examined witnesses, but neither of the defendants [those accused of wrongdoing], both of whom were laymen, had a lawyer. Phillips as chief witness for the State gave his version of the alleged robbery in detail, identifying [Pointer] as the man who had robbed him at gunpoint. Apparently Dillard tried to cross-examine Phillips, but Pointer did not, although Pointer was said to have tried to cross-examine some other witnesses at the hearing. [Pointer] was subsequently indicted on a charge of having committed the robbery. Some time before the trial was held, Phillips moved to California. After putting in evidence to show that Phillips had moved and did not intend to return to Texas, the State at the trial offered the transcript of Phillips' testimony given at the preliminary hearing as evidence against [Pointer. His] counsel immediately objected to introduction of the transcript, stating, "Your Honor, we will object to that, as it is a denial of the confrontment of the witnesses against the Defendant." Similar objections were repeatedly made by [Pointer]'s counsel, but were overruled by the trial judge, apparently in part because, as the judge viewed it, [Pointer] had been present at the preliminary hearing and therefore had been "accorded the opportunity of cross-examining the witnesses there against him." The Texas Court of Criminal Appeals, the highest state court to which the case could be taken, affirmed [upheld Pointer]'s conviction, rejecting his contention that use of the transcript to convict him denied him rights guaranteed by the Sixth and Fourteenth Amendments. We granted certiorari [agreed to hear the case] to consider the important constitutional question the case involves.

In this Court, we do not find it necessary to decide one aspect of the question [Pointer] raises, that is, whether failure to appoint counsel to represent him at the preliminary hearing unconstitutionally denied him the assistance of counsel within the meaning of *Gideon v. Wainwright*. . . . In this case, the objections and arguments in the trial court, as well as the arguments in the Court of Criminal Appeals and before us, make it clear that [Pointer]'s objection is based not so much on the fact that he had no lawyer when Phillips made his statement at the preliminary hearing as on the fact that use of the transcript of that statement at the trial denied [him] any opportunity to have the benefit of counsel's cross-examination of the principal witness against him. It is that latter question which we decide here.

The Sixth Amendment is a part of what is called our Bill of Rights. In *Gideon v. Wainwright*, in which this Court held that the Sixth Amendment's right to the assistance of counsel is obligatory upon the States, we did so on the ground that "a provision of the Bill of Rights which is 'fundamental and essential to a fair trial' is made obligatory upon the States by the Fourteenth Amendment." And last Term in *Malloy v. Hogan*, in holding that the Fifth Amendment's guarantee against self-incrimination was made applicable to the States by the Fourteenth, we reiterated the holding of *Gideon* that the Sixth Amendment's right-to-counsel guarantee is "a fundamental right, essential to a fair trial," and "thus was made obligatory on the States by the Fourteenth Amendment." We hold today that the Sixth Amendment's right of an accused to confront the witnesses against him is likewise a fundamental right and is made obligatory on the States by the Fourteenth Amendment.

It cannot seriously be doubted at this late date that the right of cross-examination is included in the right of an accused in a criminal case to confront the witnesses against him. And probably no one, certainly no one experienced in the trial of lawsuits, would deny the value of cross-examination in exposing falsehood and bringing out the truth in the trial of a criminal case. The fact that this right appears in the Sixth Amendment of our Bill of Rights reflects the belief of the Framers of those liberties and safeguards that confrontation was a fundamental right essential to a fair trial in a criminal prosecution. Moreover, the decisions of this Court and other courts throughout the years have constantly emphasized the necessity for cross-examination as a protection for defendants in criminal cases. This Court in *Kirby v. United States* referred to the right of confrontation as "[o]ne of the fundamental guarantees of life and liberty," and "a right long deemed so essential for the due protection of life and liberty that it is guarded against legislative and judicial action by provisions in the Constitution of the United States and in the constitutions of most if not of all the States composing the Union." Justice Stone, writing for the Court in *Alford v. United States*, declared that the right of cross-examination is "one of the safeguards essential to a fair trial." And, in speaking of confrontation and cross-examination, this Court said in *Greene v. McElroy:*

> "They have ancient roots. They find expression in the Sixth Amendment which provides that, in all criminal cases the accused shall enjoy the right 'to be confronted with the witnesses against him.' This Court has been zealous to protect these rights from erosion."

There are few subjects, perhaps, upon which this Court and other courts have been more nearly unanimous than in their expressions of belief that the right of confrontation and cross-examination is an essential and fundamental requirement for the kind of fair trial which is this country's constitutional goal. Indeed, we have expressly declared that to deprive an accused of the right to cross-examine the witnesses against him is a denial of the Fourteenth Amendment's guarantee of due process of law. In *In re Oliver* this Court said, "A person's right to reasonable notice of a charge against him, and an opportunity to be heard in his defense - a right to his day in court - are basic in our system of jurisprudence, and these rights include, as a minimum, a right to examine the witnesses against him, to offer testimony, and to be represented by counsel."

And earlier this Term in *Turner v. Louisiana* we held, "In the constitutional sense, trial by jury in a criminal case necessarily implies at the very least that the 'evidence developed' against a defendant shall come from the witness stand in a public courtroom where there is full judicial protection of the defendant's right of confrontation, of cross-examination, and of counsel."

We are aware that some cases, particularly *West v. Louisiana*, have stated that the Sixth Amendment's right of confrontation does not apply to trials in state courts, on the ground that the entire Sixth Amendment does not so apply. But of course since *Gideon v. Wainwright* it no longer can broadly be said that the Sixth Amendment does not apply to state courts. And as this Court said in *Malloy v. Hogan*, "The Court has not hesitated to reexamine past decisions according the Fourteenth Amendment a less central role in the preservation of basic liberties than that which was contemplated by its Framers when they added the Amendment to our constitutional scheme." . . . [T]he statements made in *West* and similar cases generally declaring that the Sixth Amendment does not apply to the States can no longer be regarded as the law. We hold that [Pointer] was entitled to be tried in accordance with the protection of the confrontation guarantee of the Sixth Amendment, and that that guarantee, like the right against compelled self-incrimination, is "to be enforced against the States under the Fourteenth Amendment according to the same standards that protect those personal rights against federal encroachment."

Under this Court's prior decisions, the Sixth Amendment's guarantee of confrontation and cross-examination was unquestionably denied [Pointer] in this case. As has been pointed out, a major reason underlying the constitutional confrontation rule is to give a defendant charged with crime an opportunity to cross-examine the witnesses against him. This Court has recognized the admissibility against an accused of dying declarations, and of testimony of a deceased witness who has testified at a former trial. Nothing we hold here is to the contrary. The case before us would be quite a different one had Phillips' statement been taken at a full-fledged hearing at which [Pointer] had been represented by counsel who had been given a complete and adequate opportunity to cross-examine. There are other analogous situations which might not fall within the scope of the constitutional rule requiring confrontation of witnesses. The case before us, however, does not present any situation like those mentioned above or others analogous to them. Because the transcript of Phillips' statement offered against [Pointer] at his trial had not been taken at a time and under circumstances affording [Pointer] through counsel an adequate opportunity to cross-examine Phillips, its introduction in a federal court in a criminal case against Pointer would have amounted to denial of the privilege of confrontation guaranteed by the Sixth Amendment. Since we hold that the right of an accused to be confronted with the witnesses against him must be determined by the same standards whether the right is denied in a federal or state proceeding, it follows that use of the transcript to convict [Pointer] denied him a constitutional right, and that his conviction must be reversed.

Reversed and remanded [returned to the lower court].

The Right To Remain Silent
Miranda v. Arizona

You are under arrest. You have the right to remain silent. Any statement you do make may be used as evidence against you. You have the right to consult with an attorney and to have one present during police questioning. If you cannot afford an attorney one will be provided for you. Do you understand your rights?   **- The Miranda Warning**

On March 13, 1963 Phoenix, Arizona police arrested Ernesto Miranda on charges of kidnapping and rape. The victim identified Miranda in a line-up. The police, without advising Miranda that he had the Constitutional right to remain silent and the right to have an attorney present during questioning, took him into an interrogation room. After two hours, the police obtained a signed confession from Miranda. He also signed a waiver stating that his confession had been made voluntarily, without threats or promises of immunity, and "with full knowledge of my legal rights, understanding any statement I make may be used against me."

At his trial, Miranda's confession and waiver of his Constitutional rights were admitted into evidence against him. Found guilty, Miranda was sentenced to 20 to 30 years' imprisonment. Miranda appealed to the Arizona Supreme Court, which affirmed his conviction and sentence.

Miranda then appealed to the United States Supreme Court. His argument was based on the inadmissibility of his confession - the police would not have obtained this self-incriminating evidence or a waiver of his Constitutional rights if (1) he had been informed of his right to remain silent and/or (2) he had been informed of his right to have an attorney present at his questioning.

On June 13, 1966 the 9-0 decision of the United States Supreme Court was announced by Chief Justice Earl Warren.

The *Miranda* Court

Chief Justice Earl Warren
Appointed Chief Justice by President Eisenhower
Served 1953 - 1969

Associate Justice Hugo Black
Appointed by President Franklin Roosevelt
Served 1937 - 1971

Associate Justice William Douglas
Appointed by President Franklin Roosevelt
Served 1939 - 1975

Associate Justice Tom Clark
Appointed by President Truman
Served 1949 - 1967

Associate Justice John Marshall Harlan
Appointed by President Eisenhower
Served 1955 - 1971

Associate Justice William Brennan
Appointed by President Eisenhower
Served 1956 - 1990

Associate Justice Potter Stewart
Appointed by President Eisenhower
Served 1958 - 1981

Associate Justice Byron White
Appointed by President Kennedy
Served 1962 - 1993

Associate Justice Arthur Goldberg
Appointed by President Kennedy
Served 1962 - 1965

The legal text of *Miranda v. Arizona* can be found in volume 384
of *United States Reports*. Our edited text follows.

MIRANDA *v.* ARIZONA
June 13, 1966

CHIEF JUSTICE EARL WARREN: The [case] before us raise[s] questions which go to the roots of our concepts of American criminal jurisprudence: the restraints society must observe consistent with the Federal Constitution in prosecuting individuals for crime. More specifically, we deal with the admissibility of statements obtained from an individual who is subjected to custodial police interrogation and the necessity for procedures which assure that the individual is accorded his privilege under the Fifth Amendment to the Constitution not to be compelled to incriminate himself.

We dealt with certain phases of this problem recently in *Escobedo v. Illinois.* There . . . law enforcement officials took the defendant into custody and interrogated him in a police station for the purpose of obtaining a confession. The police did not effectively advise him of his right to remain silent or of his right to consult with his attorney. Rather, they confronted him with an alleged accomplice who accused him of having perpetrated a murder. When the defendant [Escobedo] denied the accusation and said "I didn't shoot Manuel, you did it," they handcuffed him and took him to an interrogation room. There, while handcuffed and standing, he was questioned for four hours until he confessed. During this interrogation, the police denied his request to speak to his attorney, and they prevented his retained attorney, who had come to the police station, from consulting with him. At his trial, the State, over his objection, introduced the confession against him. We held that the statements thus made were constitutionally inadmissible.

This case has been the subject of judicial interpretation and spirited legal debate since it was decided two years ago. Both state and federal courts, in assessing its implications, have arrived at varying conclusions. . . . We granted certiorari [agreed to hear the case] to explore some facets of the problems . . . of applying the privilege against self-incrimination to in-custody interrogation, and to give concrete constitutional guidelines for law enforcement agencies and courts to follow.

. . . . We have undertaken a thorough re-examination of the *Escobedo* decision and the principles it announced, and we reaffirm [uphold] it. That case was but an explication of basic rights that are enshrined in our Constitution - that "No person . . . shall be compelled in any criminal case to be a witness against himself," and that "the accused shall . . . have the Assistance of Counsel" - rights which were put in jeopardy in that case through official overbearing. These precious rights were fixed in our Constitution only after centuries of persecution and struggle. And, in the words of Chief Justice Marshall, they were secured "for ages to come, and . . . designed to approach immortality as nearly as human institutions can approach it."

Over 70 years ago, our predecessors on this Court eloquently stated:

" . . . . While the admissions or confessions of the prisoner, when voluntarily and freely made, have always ranked high in the scale of incriminating evidence, if an accused person be asked to explain his apparent connection with a crime under investigation, the ease with which the questions put to him may assume an inquisitorial character, the temptation to press the witness unduly, to browbeat him if he be timid or reluctant, to push him into a corner, and to entrap him into fatal contradictions, which is so painfully evident in many . . . earlier state trials . . . made the system so odious as to give rise to a demand for its total abolition. The change in the English criminal procedure in that particular seems to be founded upon . . . a general and silent acquiescence of the courts in a popular demand. But, however adopted, it has become firmly embedded in English as well as in American jurisprudence. So deeply did the iniquities of the ancient system impress themselves upon the minds of the American colonists that the States, with one accord, made a denial of the right to question an accused person a part of their fundamental law. . . ."

In stating the obligation of the judiciary to apply these constitutional rights, this Court declared in *Weems v. United States*:

" . . . our contemplation cannot be only of what has been but of what may be. . . . Rights declared in words might be lost in reality. And this has been recognized. The meaning and vitality of the Constitution have developed against narrow and restrictive construction."

This was the spirit in which we delineated, in meaningful language, the manner in which the constitutional rights of the individual could be enforced against overzealous police practices. It was necessary in *Escobedo*, as here, to insure that what was proclaimed in the Constitution had not become but a "form of words" in the hands of government officials. And it is in this spirit, consistent with our role as judges, that we adhere to the principles of *Escobedo* today.

Our holding will be spelled out with some specificity in the pages which follow but briefly stated it is this: the prosecution may not use statements, whether exculpatory [clearing of guilt] or inculpatory [incriminating], stemming from custodial interrogation of the defendant unless it demonstrates the use of procedural safeguards effective to secure the privilege against self-incrimination. By custodial interrogation, we mean questioning initiated by law enforcement officers after a person has been taken into custody or otherwise deprived of his freedom of action in any significant way. As for the procedural safeguards to be employed, unless other fully effective means are devised to inform accused persons of their right of silence and to assure a continuous opportunity to exercise it, the following measures are required. Prior to any questioning, the person must be warned that he has a right to remain silent, that any statement he does make may be used as evidence against him, and that he has a right to the presence of an attorney, either retained or appointed. The defendant may waive effectuation of these rights, provided the waiver is made voluntarily, knowingly and intelligently. If, however, he indicates in any manner and at any stage of the process that he wishes to consult with an attorney before speaking there can be no questioning. Likewise, if the individual is alone and indicates in any manner that he does not wish to be interrogated, the police may not question him. The mere fact that he may have answered some questions or volunteered some statements on his own does not deprive him of the right to refrain from answering any further inquiries until he has consulted with an attorney and thereafter consents to be questioned.

The constitutional issue we decide in [this case] is the admissibility of statements obtained from a defendant questioned while in custody or otherwise deprived of his freedom of action in any significant way. . . . [Miranda] was questioned . . . in a room in which he was cut off from the outside world. [Nor] was [he] given a full and effective warning of his rights at the outset of the interrogation process. . . . [T]he questioning elicited [an] oral [admission] . . . which w[as] admitted at [trial. There was] . . . incommunicado interrogation . . . in a police-dominated atmosphere, resulting in [a] self-incriminating [statement] without full [warning] of constitutional rights.

An understanding of the nature and setting of this in-custody interrogation is essential to our decisions today. The difficulty in depicting what transpires at such interrogations stems from the fact that in this country they have largely taken place incommunicado. From extensive factual studies undertaken in the early 1930's, including the famous Wickersham Report to Congress by a Presidential Commission, it is clear that police violence and the "third degree" flourished at that time. In a series of cases decided by this Court long after these studies, the police resorted to physical brutality - beating, hanging, whipping - and to sustained and protracted questioning incommunicado in order to extort confessions. The Commission on Civil Rights in 1961 found much evidence to indicate that "some policemen still resort to physical force to obtain confessions." The use of physical brutality and violence is not, unfortunately, relegated to the past or to any part of the country. Only recently in Kings County, New York, the police brutally beat, kicked and placed lighted cigarette butts on the back of a potential witness under interrogation for the purpose of securing a statement incriminating a third party.

. . . . Again we stress that the modern practice of in-custody interrogation is psychologically rather than physically oriented. As we have stated before, " . . . [T]his Court has recognized that coercion can be mental as well as physical, and that the blood of the accused is not the only hallmark of an unconstitutional inquisition." Interrogation still takes place in privacy. Privacy results in secrecy and this in turn results in a gap in our knowledge as to what in fact goes on in the interrogation rooms. A valuable source of information about present police practices, however, may be found in various police manuals and texts which document procedures employed with success in the past, and which recommend various other effective tactics. These texts are used by law enforcement agencies themselves as guides. It should be noted that these texts professedly present the most enlightened and effective means presently used to obtain statements through custodial interrogation. By considering these texts and other data, it is possible to describe procedures observed and noted around the country.

The officers are told by the manuals that the "principal psychological factor contributing to a successful interrogation is privacy - being alone with the person under interrogation." The efficacy of this tactic has been explained as follows:

"If at all practicable, the interrogation should take place in the investigator's office or at least in a room of his own choice. The subject should be deprived of every psychological advantage. In his own home he may be confident, indignant, or recalcitrant. He is more keenly aware of his rights and more reluctant to tell of his indiscretions or criminal behavior within the walls of his home. Moreover his family and other friends are nearby, their presence lending moral support. In his own office, the investigator possesses all the advantages. The atmosphere suggests the invincibility of the forces of the law."

To highlight the isolation and unfamiliar surroundings, the manuals instruct the police to display an air of confidence in the suspect's guilt and from outward appearance to maintain only an interest in confirming certain details. The guilt of the subject is to be posited as a fact. The interrogator should direct his comments toward the reasons why the subject committed the act, rather than court failure by asking the subject whether he did it. Like other men, perhaps the subject has had a bad family life, had an unhappy childhood, had too much to drink, had an unrequited desire for women. The officers are instructed to minimize the moral seriousness of the offense, to cast blame on the victim or on society. These tactics are designed to put the subject in a psychological state where his story is but an elaboration of what the police purport to know already - that he is guilty. Explanations to the contrary are dismissed and discouraged.

The texts thus stress that the major qualities an interrogator should possess are patience and perseverance. One writer describes the efficacy of these characteristics in this manner:

"In the preceding paragraphs emphasis has been placed on kindness and stratagems. The investigator will, however, encounter many situations where the sheer weight of his personality will be the deciding factor. Where emotional appeals and tricks are employed to no avail, he must rely on an oppressive atmosphere of dogged persistence. He must interrogate steadily and without relent, leaving the subject no prospect of surcease. He must dominate his subject and overwhelm him with his inexorable will to obtain the truth. He should interrogate for a spell of several hours pausing only for the subject's necessities in acknowledgment of the need to avoid a charge of duress that can be technically substantiated. In a serious case, the interrogation may continue for days, with the required intervals for food and sleep, but with no respite from the atmosphere of domination. It is possible in this way to induce the subject to talk without resorting to duress or coercion. The method should be used only when the guilt of the subject appears highly probable."

The manuals suggest that the suspect be offered legal excuses for his actions in order to obtain an initial admission of guilt. Where there is a suspected revenge killing, for example, the interrogator may say:

"Joe, you probably didn't go out looking for this fellow with the purpose of shooting him. My guess is, however, that you expected something from him and that's why you carried a gun - for your own protection. You knew him for what he was, no good. Then when you met him he probably started using foul, abusive language and he gave some indication that he was about to pull a gun on you, and that's when you had to act to save your own life. That's about it, isn't it, Joe?"

Having then obtained the admission of shooting, the interrogator is advised to refer to circumstantial evidence which negates the self-defense explanation. This should enable him to secure the entire story. One text notes that, "Even if he fails to do so, the inconsistency between the subject's original denial of the shooting and his present admission of at least doing the shooting will serve to deprive him of a self-defense 'out' at the time of trial."

When the techniques described above prove unavailing, the texts recommend they be alternated with a show of some hostility. One ploy often used has been termed the "friendly-unfriendly," or the "Mutt and Jeff" act:

". . . In this technique, two agents are employed. Mutt, the relentless investigator, who knows the subject is guilty and is not going to waste any time. He's sent a dozen men away for this crime, and he's going to send the subject away for the full term. Jeff, on the other hand, is obviously a kindhearted man. He has a family himself. He has a brother who was involved in a little scrape like this. He disapproves of Mutt and his tactics and will arrange to get him off the case if the subject will cooperate. He can't hold Mutt off for very long. The subject would be wise to make a quick decision. The technique is applied by having both investigators present while Mutt acts out his role. Jeff may stand by quietly and demur at some of Mutt's tactics. When Jeff makes his plea for cooperation, Mutt is not present in the room."

The interrogators sometimes are instructed to induce a confession out of trickery. The technique here is quite effective in crimes which require identification or which run in series. In the identification situation, the interrogator may take a break in his questioning to place the subject among a group of men in a line-up. "The witness or complainant (previously coached, if necessary) studies the line-up and confidently points out the subject as the guilty party." Then the questioning resumes "as though there were now no doubt about the guilt of the subject." A variation on this technique is called the "reverse line-up":

"The accused is placed in a line-up, but this time he is identified by several fictitious witnesses or victims who associated him with different offenses. It is expected that the subject will become desperate and confess to the offense under investigation in order to escape from the false accusations."

The manuals also contain instructions for police on how to handle the individual who refuses to discuss the matter entirely, or who asks for an attorney or relatives. The examiner is to concede him the right to remain silent. "This usually has a very undermining effect. First of all, he is disappointed in his expectation of an unfavorable reaction on the part of the interrogator. Secondly, a concession of this right to remain silent impresses the subject with the apparent fairness of his interrogator." After this psychological conditioning, however, the officer is told to point out the incriminating significance of the suspect's refusal to talk:

"Joe, you have a right to remain silent. That's your privilege and I'm the last person in the world who'll try to take it away from you. If that's the way you want to leave this, O. K. But let me ask you this. Suppose you were in my shoes and I were in yours and you called me in to ask me about this and I told you, 'I don't want to answer any of your questions.' You'd think I had something to hide, and you'd probably be right in thinking that. That's exactly what I'll have to think about you, and so will everybody else. So let's sit here and talk this whole thing over."

Few will persist in their initial refusal to talk, it is said, if this monologue is employed correctly.

In the event that the subject wishes to speak to a relative or an attorney, the following advice is tendered:

"[T]he interrogator should respond by suggesting that the subject first tell the truth to the interrogator himself rather than get anyone else involved in the matter. If the request is for an attorney, the interrogator may suggest that the subject save himself or his family the expense of any such professional service, particularly if he is innocent of the offense under investigation. The interrogator may also add, 'Joe, I'm only looking for the truth, and if you're telling the truth, that's it. You can handle this by yourself.'"

From these representative samples of interrogation techniques, the setting prescribed by the manuals and observed in practice becomes clear. In essence, it is this: To be alone with the subject is essential to prevent distraction and to deprive him of any outside support. The aura of confidence in his guilt undermines his will to resist. He merely confirms the preconceived story the police seek to have him describe. Patience and persistence, at times relentless questioning, are employed. To obtain a confession, the interrogator must "patiently maneuver himself or his quarry into a position from which the desired objective may be attained." When normal procedures fail to produce the needed result, the police may resort to deceptive stratagems such as giving false legal advice. It is important to keep the subject off balance, for example, by trading on his insecurity about himself or his surroundings. The police then persuade, trick, or cajole him out of exercising his constitutional rights.

Even without employing brutality, the "third degree" or the specific stratagems described above, the very fact of custodial interrogation exacts a heavy toll on individual liberty, and trades on the weakness of individuals. . . .

[T]oday . . . we concern ourselves primarily with this interrogation atmosphere and the evils it can bring. In *Miranda v. Arizona,* the police arrested the defendant and took him to a special interrogation room, where they secured a confession. . . .

[T]he defendant was thrust into an unfamiliar atmosphere and run through menacing police interrogation procedures. The potentiality for compulsion is forcefully apparent, for example . . . where the indigent Mexican defendant was a seriously disturbed individual with pronounced sexual fantasies. . . . To be sure, the records do not evince overt physical coercion or patent psychological ploys. The fact remains that . . . the officers [did not] undertake to afford appropriate safeguards at the outset of the interrogation to insure that the statements were truly the product of free choice.

. . . . From the foregoing, we can readily perceive an intimate connection between the privilege against self-incrimination and police custodial questioning. It is fitting to turn to history and precedent [a rule of law established by prior cases] underlying the Self-Incrimination Clause to determine its applicability in this situation.

. . . . [W]e hold that when an individual is taken into custody or otherwise deprived of his freedom by the authorities in any significant way and is subjected to questioning, the privilege against self-incrimination is jeopardized. Procedural safeguards must be employed to protect the privilege, and unless other fully effective means are adopted to notify the person of his right of silence and to assure that the exercise of the right will be scrupulously honored, the following measures are required. He must be warned prior to any questioning that he has the right to remain silent, that anything he says can be used against him in a court of law, that he has the right to the presence of an attorney, and that if he cannot afford an attorney one will be appointed for him prior to any questioning if he so desires. Opportunity to exercise these rights must be afforded to him throughout the interrogation. After such warnings have been given, and such opportunity afforded him, the individual may knowingly and intelligently waive these rights and agree to answer questions or make a statement. But unless and until such warnings and waiver are demonstrated by the prosecution at trial, no evidence obtained as a result of interrogation can be used against him.

A recurrent argument . . . is that society's need for interrogation outweighs the privilege. This argument is not unfamiliar to this Court. The whole thrust of our foregoing discussion demonstrates that the Constitution has prescribed the rights of the individual when confronted with the power of government when it provided in the Fifth Amendment that an individual cannot be compelled to be a witness against himself. That right cannot be abridged. As Justice Brandeis once observed:

> "Decency, security and liberty alike demand that government officials shall be subjected to the same rules of conduct that are commands to the citizen. In a government of laws, existence of the government will be imperiled if it fails to observe the law scrupulously. Our Government is the potent, the omnipresent teacher. For good or for ill, it teaches the whole people by its example. Crime is contagious. If the Government becomes a lawbreaker, it breeds contempt for law; it invites every man to become a law unto himself; it invites anarchy. To declare that in the administration of the criminal law the end justifies the means . . . would bring terrible retribution. Against that pernicious doctrine this Court should resolutely set its face. . . ."

In this connection, one of our country's distinguished jurists has pointed out, "The quality of a nation's civilization can be largely measured by the methods it uses in the enforcement of its criminal law."

If the individual desires to exercise his privilege, he has the right to do so. This is not for the authorities to decide. An attorney may advise his client not to talk to police until he has had an opportunity to investigate the case, or he may wish to be present with his client during any police questioning. In doing so an attorney is merely exercising the good professional judgment he has been taught. This is not cause for considering the attorney a menace to law enforcement. He is merely carrying out what he is sworn to do under his oath - to protect to the extent of his ability the rights of his client. In fulfilling this responsibility the attorney plays a vital role in the administration of criminal justice under our Constitution.

In announcing these principles, we are not unmindful of the burdens which law enforcement officials must bear, often under trying circumstances. We also fully recognize the obligation of all citizens to aid in enforcing the criminal laws. This Court, while protecting individual rights, has always given ample latitude to law enforcement agencies in the legitimate exercise of their duties. The limits we have placed on the interrogation process should not constitute an undue interference with a proper system of law enforcement. As we have noted, our decision does not in any way preclude police from carrying out their traditional investigatory functions. . . .

Because of the nature of the problem and because of its recurrent significance in numerous cases, we have to this point discussed the relationship of the Fifth Amendment privilege to police interrogation without specific concentration on the facts. . . . We turn now to these facts to consider the application . . . of the constitutional principles discussed above. . . . [W]e have concluded that statements were obtained from the defendant under circumstances that did not meet constitutional standards for protection of the privilege.

. . . On March 13, 1963, petitioner, Ernesto Miranda, was arrested at his home and taken in custody to a Phoenix police station. He was there identified by the complaining witness. The police then took him to "Interrogation Room No. 2" of the detective bureau. There he was questioned by two police officers. The officers admitted at trial that Miranda was not advised that he had a right to have an attorney present. Two hours later, the officers emerged from the interrogation room with a written confession signed by Miranda. At the top of the statement was a typed paragraph stating that the confession was made voluntarily, without threats or promises of immunity and "with full knowledge of my legal rights, understanding any statement I make may be used against me."

At his trial before a jury, the written confession was admitted into evidence over the objection of defense counsel, and the officers testified to the prior oral confession made by Miranda during the interrogation. Miranda was found guilty of kidnapping and rape. He was sentenced to 20 to 30 years' imprisonment on each count, the sentences to run concurrently. On appeal, the Supreme Court of Arizona held that Miranda's constitutional rights were not violated in obtaining the confession, and affirmed the conviction. In reaching its decision, the court emphasized heavily the fact that Miranda did not specifically request counsel.

We reverse. From the testimony of the officers and by the admission of [Miranda], it is clear that [he] was not in any way apprised of his right to consult with an attorney and to have one present during the interrogation, nor was his right not to be compelled to incriminate himself effectively protected in any other manner. Without these warnings the statements were inadmissible. The mere fact that he signed a statement which contained a typed-in clause stating that he had "full knowledge" of his "legal rights" does not approach the knowing and intelligent waiver required to relinquish constitutional rights. . . .

Preventive Detention
United States v. Salerno

No person shall . . . be deprived of life, liberty, or property without due process of law. **- The Fifth Amendment**

On October 12, 1984 the U.S. Congress enacted the Bail Reform Act. The Act allowed Federal Judges, after a hearing, to indefinitely detain a person arrested, but not yet tried, for a federal crime, if the judge decides that the person poses a continuing threat to the community.

On March 21, 1986 Anthony "Fat Tony" Salerno, head of New York City's Genovese Organized Crime Family, was arrested by federal authorities on an indictment which charged him with multiple violations of the federal Racketeer Influenced and Corrupt Organizations Act. At his arraignment, the U.S. Justice Department requested that Salerno, whom they believed to be a continuing threat to the community, be held without bail in indefinite pre-trial custody, pursuant to the Bail Act. After a hearing, Federal Judge John Walker, Jr. ordered Salerno to be detained, stating, *The activities of a criminal organization such as the Genovese Family do not cease with the arrest of its principals and their release on even the most stringent of bail conditions. The illegal businesses, in place for many years, require constant attention and protection, or they will fail. Under these circumstances, this court recognizes a strong incentive on the part of its leadership to continue business as usual. When business as usual involves threats, beatings, and murder, the present danger such people pose in the community is self-evident.*

The U.S. Court of Appeals overturned the District Court's pre-trial detention ruling as a violation of Salerno's rights under the Fifth Amendment's Due Process Clause. The Justice Department appealed to the United States Supreme Court. On May 26, 1987 the 6-3 decision of the United States Supreme Court was announced by Chief Justice William Rehnquist.

The *Salerno* Court

Chief Justice William Rehnquist
Appointed Associate Justice by President Nixon
Appointed Chief Justice by President Reagan
Served 1971 -

Associate Justice William Brennan
Appointed by President Eisenhower
Served 1956 - 1990

Associate Justice Byron White
Appointed by President Kennedy
Served 1962 - 1993

Associate Justice Thurgood Marshall
Appointed by President Lyndon Johnson
Served 1967 - 1991

Associate Justice Harry Blackmun
Appointed by President Nixon
Served 1970 - 1994

Associate Justice Lewis Powell
Appointed by President Nixon
Served 1971 - 1987

Associate Justice John Paul Stevens
Appointed by President Ford
Served 1975 -

Associate Justice Sandra Day O'Connor
Appointed by President Reagan
Served 1981 -

Associate Justice Antonin Scalia
Appointed by President Reagan
Served 1986 -

The legal text of *United States v. Salerno* can be found in volume 481 of *United States Reports*. Our edited text follows.

UNITED STATES *v.* SALERNO
May 26, 1987

CHIEF JUSTICE WILLIAM REHNQUIST: The Bail Reform Act of 1984 allows a federal court to detain an arrestee pending trial if the Government demonstrates by clear and convincing evidence after an adversary hearing that no release conditions "will reasonably assure . . . the safety of any other person and the community." The United States Court of Appeals . . . struck down this provision of the Act as . . . unconstitutional, because, in that court's words, this type of pretrial detention violates "substantive [essential] due process." We granted certiorari [agreed to hear the case] because of a conflict among the Courts of Appeals regarding the validity of the Act. We hold that . . . the Act fully comports with constitutional requirements. We therefore reverse.

Responding to "the alarming problem of crimes committed by persons on release" Congress formulated the Bail Reform Act of 1984 as the solution to a bail crisis in the federal courts. The Act represents the National Legislature's considered response to numerous perceived deficiencies in the federal bail process. By providing for sweeping changes in both the way federal courts consider bail applications and the circumstances under which bail is granted, Congress hoped to "give the courts adequate authority to make release decisions that give appropriate recognition to the danger a person may pose to others if released."

To this end . . . [the Bail] Act requires a judicial officer to determine whether an arrestee shall be detained . . . [and] provides that "[i]f, after a hearing . . . the judicial officer finds that no condition or combination of conditions will reasonably assure the appearance of the person as required and the safety of any other person and the community, he shall order the detention of the person prior to trial." [The Bail Act] provides the arrestee with a number of procedural safeguards. He may request the presence of counsel at the detention hearing, he may testify and present witnesses in his behalf, as well as proffer evidence, and he may cross-examine other witnesses appearing at the hearing. If the judicial officer finds that no conditions of pretrial release can reasonably assure the safety of other persons and the community, he must state his findings of fact in writing, and support his conclusion with "clear and convincing evidence."

The judicial officer is not given unbridled discretion in making the detention determination. Congress has specified the considerations relevant to that decision. These factors include the nature and seriousness of the charges, the substantiality of the Government's evidence against the arrestee, the arrestee's background and characteristics, and the nature and seriousness of the danger posed by the suspect's release. Should a judicial officer order detention, the detainee is entitled to expedited appellate review of the detention order.

. . . Anthony Salerno . . . [was] arrested on March 21, 1986, after being charged in a 29-count indictment [charge] alleging various Racketeer Influenced and Corrupt Organizations Act (RICO) violations, mail and wire fraud offenses, extortion, and various criminal gambling violations. The RICO counts alleged 35 acts of racketeering activity, including fraud, extortion, gambling, and conspiracy to commit murder. At [Salerno's] arraignment [appearance in court to enter a plea of guilty or innocent], the Government moved to have [him] . . . detained pursuant to [the Bail Act], on the ground that no condition of release would assure the safety of the community or any person. The District Court held a hearing at which the Government made a detailed proffer of evidence. The Government's case showed that Salerno was the "boss" of the Genovese crime family of La Cosa Nostra. . . . According to the Government's proffer, based in large part on conversations intercepted by a court-ordered wiretap, [Salerno] had participated in wide-ranging conspiracies to aid [his] illegitimate enterprises through violent means. The Government also offered the testimony of two of its trial witnesses, who would assert that Salerno personally participated in two murder conspiracies. Salerno . . . challeng[ed] the credibility of the Government's witnesses. He offered the testimony of several character witnesses, as well as a letter from his doctor stating that he was suffering from a serious medical condition. . . .

The District Court granted the Government's detention motion, concluding that the Government had established by clear and convincing evidence that no condition or combination of conditions of release would ensure the safety of the community or any person:

"The activities of a criminal organization such as the Genovese Family do not cease with the arrest of its principals and their release on even the most stringent of bail conditions. The illegal businesses, in place for many years, require constant attention and protection, or they will fail. Under these circumstances, this court recognizes a strong incentive on the part of its leadership to continue business as usual. When business as usual involves threats, beatings, and murder, the present danger such people pose in the community is self-evident."

[Salerno] appealed, contending that to the extent that the [Bail Act] permits pretrial detention on the ground that the arrestee is likely to commit future crimes, it is unconstitutional. . . . Over a dissent, the United States Court of Appeals . . . agreed. Although the court agreed that pretrial detention could be imposed if the defendants [persons accused of wrongdoing] were likely to intimidate witnesses or otherwise jeopardize the trial process, it found [the Bail Act's] "authorization of pretrial detention [on the ground of future dangerousness] repugnant to the concept of substantive due process, which we believe prohibits the total deprivation of liberty simply as a means of preventing future crimes." The [Court of Appeals] concluded that the Government could not, consistent with due process, detain persons who had not been accused of any crime merely because they were thought to present a danger to the community. It reasoned that our criminal law system holds persons accountable for past actions, not anticipated future actions. Although a court could detain an arrestee who threatened to flee before trial, such detention would be permissible because it would serve the basic objective of a criminal system - bringing the accused to trial. The court distinguished [applied] our decision in *Gerstein v. Pugh*, in which we upheld police detention pursuant to arrest. The court construed [interpreted] *Gerstein* as limiting such detention to the "administrative steps incident to arrest." The Court of Appeals also found our decision in *Schall v. Martin*, upholding postarrest pretrial detention of juveniles, inapposite because juveniles have a lesser interest in liberty than do adults. The dissenting judge concluded that . . . the Bail Reform Act adequately balanced the Federal Government's compelling interests in public safety against the detainee's liberty interests.

. . . . The fact that the Bail Reform Act might operate unconstitutionally under some conceivable set of circumstances is insufficient to render it wholly invalid. . . . We think [Salerno has] failed to shoulder their heavy burden to demonstrate that the Act is . . . unconstitutional.

[Salerno] present[s] two grounds for invalidating the Bail Reform Act's provisions permitting pretrial detention on the basis of future dangerousness. First, [he relies] upon the Court of Appeals' conclusion that the Act exceeds the limitations placed upon the Federal Government by the Due Process Clause of the Fifth Amendment. Second, [he] contend[s] that the Act contravenes [is inconsistent with] the Eighth Amendment's proscription [prohibition] against excessive bail. We treat these contentions in turn.

The Due Process Clause of the Fifth Amendment provides that "No person shall . . . be deprived of life, liberty, or property, without due process of law. . . ." This Court has held that the Due Process Clause protects individuals against two types of government action. So-called "substantive due process" prevents the government from engaging in conduct that "shocks the conscience," or interferes with rights "implicit in the concept of ordered liberty." When government action depriving a person of life, liberty, or property survives substantive due process scrutiny, it must still be implemented in a fair manner. This requirement has traditionally been referred to as "procedural" due process.

[Salerno] first argue[s] that the Act violates substantive due process because the pretrial detention it authorizes constitutes impermissible punishment before trial. The Government, however, has never argued that pretrial detention could be upheld if it were "punishment." The Court of Appeals assumed that pretrial detention under the Bail Reform Act is regulatory, not penal, and we agree that it is.

As an initial matter, the mere fact that a person is detained does not inexorably lead to the conclusion that the government has imposed punishment. To determine whether a restriction on liberty constitutes impermissible punishment or permissible regulation, we first look to legislative intent. Unless Congress expressly intended to impose punitive restrictions, the punitive/regulatory distinction turns on "whether an alternative purpose to which [the restriction] may rationally be connected is assignable for it, and whether it appears excessive in relation to the alternative purpose assigned [to it]."

We conclude that the detention imposed by the Act falls on the regulatory side of the dichotomy. The legislative history of the Bail Reform Act clearly indicates that Congress did not formulate the pretrial detention provisions as punishment for dangerous individuals. Congress instead perceived pretrial detention as a potential solution to a pressing societal problem. There is no doubt that preventing danger to the community is a legitimate regulatory goal.

Nor are the incidents of pretrial detention excessive in relation to the regulatory goal Congress sought to achieve. The Bail Reform Act carefully limits the circumstances under which detention may be sought to the most serious of crimes [cases involving crimes of violence, offenses for which the sentence is life imprisonment or death, serious drug offenses, or certain repeat offenders]. The arrestee is entitled to a prompt detention hearing and the maximum length of pretrial detention is limited by the stringent time limitations of the Speedy Trial Act. Moreover, as in *Schall*, the conditions of confinement envisioned by the Act "appear to reflect the regulatory purposes relied upon by the" Government. As in *Schall*, the statute at issue here requires that detainees be housed in a "facility separate, to the extent practicable, from persons awaiting or serving sentences or being held in custody pending appeal." We conclude, therefore, that the pretrial detention contemplated by the Bail Reform Act is regulatory in nature, and does not constitute punishment before trial in violation of the Due Process Clause.

The Court of Appeals nevertheless concluded that "the Due Process Clause prohibits pretrial detention on the ground of danger to the community as a regulatory measure, without regard to the duration of the detention." [Salerno] characterize[s] the Due Process Clause as erecting an impenetrable "wall" in this area that "no governmental interest - rational, important, compelling or otherwise - may surmount."

We do not think the Clause lays down any such categorical imperative. We have repeatedly held that the Government's regulatory interest in community safety can, in appropriate circumstances, outweigh an individual's liberty interest. For example, in times of war or insurrection, when society's interest is at its peak, the Government may detain individuals whom the Government believes to be dangerous. Even outside the exigencies of war, we have found that sufficiently compelling governmental interests can justify detention of dangerous persons. Thus, we have found no absolute constitutional barrier to detention of potentially dangerous resident aliens pending deportation proceedings. We have also held that the government may detain mentally unstable individuals who present a danger to the public, and dangerous defendants who become incompetent to stand trial. We have approved of postarrest regulatory detention of juveniles when they present a continuing danger to the community. Even competent adults may face substantial liberty restrictions as a result of the operation of our criminal justice system. If the police suspect an individual of a crime, they may arrest and hold him until a neutral magistrate determines whether probable cause exists. Finally, [Salerno] concede[s] and the Court of Appeals noted that an arrestee may be incarcerated until trial if he presents a risk of flight, or a danger to witnesses.

[Salerno] characterize[s] all of these cases as exceptions to the "general rule" of substantive due process that the government may not detain a person prior to a judgment of guilt in a criminal trial. Such a "general rule" may freely be conceded, but we think that these cases show a sufficient number of exceptions to the rule that the congressional action challenged here can hardly be characterized as totally novel. Given the well-established authority of the government, in special circumstances, to restrain individuals' liberty prior to or even without criminal trial and conviction, we think that the present statute providing for pretrial detention on the basis of dangerousness must be evaluated in precisely the same manner that we evaluated the laws in the cases discussed above.

The government's interest in preventing crime by arrestees is both legitimate and compelling. In *Schall,* we recognized the strength of the State's interest in preventing juvenile crime. This general concern with crime prevention is no less compelling when the suspects are adults. Indeed, "[t]he harm suffered by the victim of a crime is not dependent upon the age of the perpetrator." The Bail Reform Act of 1984 responds to an even more particularized governmental interest than the interest we sustained [upheld] in *Schall.* The statute we upheld in *Schall* permitted pretrial detention of any juvenile arrested on any charge after a showing that the individual might commit some undefined further crimes. The Bail Reform Act, in contrast, narrowly focuses on a particularly acute problem in which the Government interests are overwhelming. The Act operates only on individuals who have been arrested for a specific category of extremely serious offenses. Congress specifically found that these individuals are far more likely to be responsible for dangerous acts in the community after arrest. Nor is the Act by any means a scattershot attempt to incapacitate those who are merely suspected of these serious crimes. The Government must first of all demonstrate probable cause to believe that the charged crime has been committed by the arrestee, but that is not enough. In a full-blown adversary hearing, the Government must convince a neutral decisionmaker by clear and convincing evidence that no conditions of release can reasonably assure the safety of the community or any person. While the Government's general interest in preventing crime is compelling, even this interest is heightened when the Government musters convincing proof that the arrestee, already indicted or held to answer for a serious crime, presents a demonstrable danger to the community. Under these narrow circumstances, society's interest in crime prevention is at its greatest.

On the other side of the scale, of course, is the individual's strong interest in liberty. We do not minimize the importance and fundamental nature of this right. But, as our cases hold, this right may, in circumstances where the government's interest is sufficiently weighty, be subordinated to the greater needs of society. We think that Congress' careful delineation of the circumstances under which detention will be permitted satisfies this standard. When the Government proves by clear and convincing evidence that an arrestee presents an identified and articulable threat to an individual or the community, we believe that, consistent with the Due Process Clause, a court may disable the arrestee from executing that threat. Under these circumstances, we cannot categorically state that pretrial detention "offends some principle of justice so rooted in the traditions and conscience of our people as to be ranked as fundamental."

Finally, we may dispose briefly of [Salerno's] . . . challenge to the procedures of the Bail Reform Act. To sustain them against such a challenge, we need only find them "adequate to authorize the pretrial detention of at least some [persons] charged with crimes," whether or not they might be insufficient in some particular circumstances. We think they pass that test. As we stated in *Schall,* "there is nothing inherently unattainable about a prediction of future criminal conduct."

Under the Bail Reform Act, the procedures by which a judicial officer evaluates the likelihood of future dangerousness are specifically designed to further the accuracy of that determination. Detainees have a right to counsel at the detention hearing. They may testify in their own behalf, present information by proffer or otherwise, and cross-examine witnesses who appear at the hearing. The judicial officer charged with the responsibility of determining the appropriateness of detention is guided by statutorily enumerated factors, which include the nature and the circumstances of the charges, the weight of the evidence, the history and characteristics of the putative [supposed] offender, and the danger to the community. The Government must prove its case by clear and convincing evidence. Finally, the judicial officer must include written findings of fact and a written statement of reasons for a decision to detain. The Act's review provisions provide for immediate appellate review of the detention decision.

We think these extensive safeguards suffice to repel a . . . challenge. The protections are more exacting than those we found sufficient in the juvenile context, and they far exceed what we found necessary to effect limited postarrest detention in *Gerstein*. Given the legitimate and compelling regulatory purpose of the Act and the procedural protections it offers, we conclude that the Act is not . . . invalid under the Due Process Clause of the Fifth Amendment.

[Salerno] also contend[s] that the Bail Reform Act violates the Excessive Bail Clause of the Eighth Amendment. . . .

The Eighth Amendment addresses pretrial release by providing merely that "[e]xcessive bail shall not be required." This Clause, of course, says nothing about whether bail shall be available at all. [Salerno] nevertheless contend[s] that this Clause grants [him] a right to bail calculated solely upon considerations of flight. [He relies] on *Stack v. Boyle*, in which the Court stated that "[b]ail set at a figure higher than an amount reasonably calculated [to ensure the defendant's presence at trial] is 'excessive' under the Eighth Amendment." In [Salerno's] view, since the Bail Reform Act allows a court essentially to set bail at an infinite amount for reasons not related to the risk of flight, it violates the Excessive Bail Clause. [Salerno] concede[s] that the right to bail they have discovered in the Eighth Amendment is not absolute. A court may, for example, refuse bail in capital cases [those in which the death penalty is an option]. And, as the Court of Appeals noted and [Salerno] admit[s], a court may refuse bail when the defendant presents a threat to the judicial process by intimidating witnesses. [Salerno] characterize[s] these exceptions as consistent with what they claim to be the sole purpose of bail - to ensure the integrity of the judicial process.

While we agree that a primary function of bail is to safeguard the courts' role in adjudicating [determining] the guilt or innocence of defendants, we reject the proposition that the Eighth Amendment categorically prohibits the government from pursuing other admittedly compelling interests through regulation of pretrial release. The above-quoted dictum [parts of an opinion that are not law] in *Stack* is far too slender a reed on which to rest this argument. The Court in *Stack* had no occasion to consider whether the Excessive Bail Clause requires courts to admit all defendants to bail, because the statute before the Court in that case in fact allowed the defendants to be bailed. Thus, the Court had to determine only whether bail, admittedly available in that case, was excessive if set at a sum greater than that necessary to ensure the arrestees' presence at trial.

The holding of *Stack* is illuminated by the Court's holding just four months later in *Carlson v. Landon*. In that case, remarkably similar to the [one before us], the detainees had been arrested and held without bail pending a determination of deportability. The Attorney General refused to release the individuals, "on the ground that there was reasonable cause to believe that [their] release would be prejudicial to the public interest and would endanger the welfare and safety of the United States." The detainees brought the same challenge that [Salerno] bring[s] to us today - the Eighth Amendment required them to be admitted to bail. The Court squarely rejected this proposition:

"The bail clause was lifted with slight changes from the English Bill of Rights Act. In England that clause has never been thought to accord a right to bail in all cases, but merely to provide that bail shall not be excessive in those cases where it is proper to grant bail. When this clause was carried over into our Bill of Rights, nothing was said that indicated any different concept. The Eighth Amendment has not prevented Congress from defining the classes of cases in which bail shall be allowed in this country. Thus, in criminal cases bail is not compulsory where the punishment may be death. Indeed, the very language of the Amendment fails to say all arrests must be bailable."

Carlson was a civil case [involving private rights], and we need not decide today whether the Excessive Bail Clause speaks at all to Congress' power to define the classes of criminal arrestees who shall be admitted to bail. For even if we were to conclude that the Eighth Amendment imposes some substantive limitations on the National Legislature's powers in this area, we would still hold that the Bail Reform Act is valid. Nothing in the text of the Bail Clause limits permissible Government considerations solely to questions of flight. The only arguable substantive limitation of the Bail Clause is that the Government's proposed conditions of release or detention not be "excessive" in light of the perceived evil. Of course, to determine whether the Government's response is excessive, we must compare that response against the interest the Government seeks to protect by means of that response. Thus, when the Government has admitted that its only interest is in preventing flight, bail must be set by a court at a sum designed to ensure that goal, and no more. We believe that when Congress has mandated detention on the basis of a compelling interest other than prevention of flight, as it has here, the Eighth Amendment does not require release on bail.

In our society liberty is the norm, and detention prior to trial or without trial is the carefully limited exception. We hold that the provisions for pretrial detention in the Bail Reform Act of 1984 fall within that carefully limited exception. The Act authorizes the detention prior to trial of arrestees charged with serious felonies who are found after an adversary hearing to pose a threat to the safety of individuals or to the community which no condition of release can dispel. The numerous procedural safeguards detailed above must attend this adversary hearing. We are unwilling to say that this congressional determination, based as it is upon that primary concern of every government (a concern for the safety and indeed the lives of its citizens) . . . violates either the Due Process Clause of the Fifth Amendment or the Excessive Bail Clause of the Eighth Amendment.

The judgment of the Court of Appeals is therefore reversed.

Victim Impact Statements
Booth v. Maryland

The murder of Mr. and Mrs. Bronstein is still such a shocking, painful, and devastating memory to [the Bronstein family] that it permeates every aspect of their daily lives. It is doubtful that they will ever be able to fully recover from this tragedy and not be haunted by the memory of the brutal manner in which their loved ones were murdered and taken from them.

- The Bronstein Family's Victim Impact Statement

On May 19, 1983, while robbing their West Baltimore, Maryland home, John Booth brutally murdered an elderly married couple, Irvin Bronstein, 78, and his wife, Rose, 75.

Booth was tried and convicted on two counts of first degree murder. The jury was to decide whether Booth would, on each count, receive a life or death sentence. In accordance with Maryland law (similar laws were then in effect in 36 other states), a Victim Impact Statement, a full report on the emotional and psychological effects of the murders on the victims' family, was compiled for the jury so that they fully understood who the victims were and what impact their murders had on their family.

After the jury heard the Bronstein Family's Victim Impact Statement, they sentenced Booth to death. Booth appealed to the Maryland Court of Appeals on the grounds that the Victim Impact Statement was an arbitrary factor that had prejudiced the jury's decision. Booth's essential argument was that if his victims had had no family, or if that family had not been so seriously affected by the murders, the jury would not have sentenced him to the harsher penalty. The Maryland Court rejected Booth's argument and upheld his death sentence. Booth appealed to the U.S. Supreme Court.

On June 15, 1987 the 5-4 decision of the United States Supreme Court was announced by Associate Justice Lewis Powell.

The *Booth* Court

Chief Justice William Rehnquist
Appointed Associate Justice by President Nixon
Appointed Chief Justice by President Reagan
Served 1971 -

Associate Justice William Brennan
Appointed by President Eisenhower
Served 1956 - 1990

Associate Justice Byron White
Appointed by President Kennedy
Served 1962 - 1993

Associate Justice Thurgood Marshall
Appointed by President Lyndon Johnson
Served 1967 - 1991

Associate Justice Harry Blackmun
Appointed by President Nixon
Served 1970 - 1994

Associate Justice Lewis Powell
Appointed by President Nixon
Served 1971 - 1987

Associate Justice John Paul Stevens
Appointed by President Ford
Served 1975 -

Associate Justice Sandra Day O'Connor
Appointed by President Reagan
Served 1981 -

Associate Justice Antonin Scalia
Appointed by President Reagan
Served 1986 -

The legal text of *Booth v. Maryland* can be found in volume 482 of
United States Reports. Our edited text follows.

BOOTH v. MARYLAND
June 15, 1987

JUSTICE LEWIS POWELL: The question presented is whether the Constitution prohibits a jury from considering a "victim impact statement" during the sentencing phase of a capital murder trial [one in which a death penalty may be imposed].

In 1983, Irvin Bronstein, 78, and his wife Rose, 75, were robbed and murdered in their West Baltimore home. The murderers, John Booth and Willie Reid, entered the victims' home for the apparent purpose of stealing money to buy heroin. Booth, a neighbor of the Bronsteins, knew that the elderly couple could identify him. The victims were bound and gagged, and then stabbed repeatedly in the chest with a kitchen knife. The bodies were discovered two days later by the Bronsteins' son.

A jury found Booth guilty of two counts of first-degree murder, two counts of robbery, and conspiracy to commit robbery. The prosecution requested the death penalty, and Booth elected to have his sentence determined by the jury instead of the judge. Before the sentencing phase began, the State Division of Parole and Probation (DPP) compiled a presentence report that described Booth's background, education and employment history, and criminal record. Under a Maryland statute, the presentence report in all felony cases also must include a victim impact statement (VIS), describing the effect of the crime on the victim and his family. Specifically, the report shall:

"(i) Identify the victim of the offense;
"(ii) itemize any economic loss suffered by the victim as a result of the offense;
"(iii) Identify any physical injury suffered by the victim as a result of the offense along with its seriousness and permanence;
"(iv) Describe any change in the victim's personal welfare or familial relationships as a result of the offense;
"(v) Identify any request for psychological services initiated by the victim or the victim's family as a result of the offense; and

"(vi) Contain any other information related to the impact of the offense upon the victim or the victim's family that the trial court requires."

Although the VIS is compiled by the DPP, the information is supplied by the victim or the victim's family. The VIS may be read to the jury during the sentencing phase, or the family members may be called to testify as to the information.

The VIS in Booth's case was based on interviews with the Bronsteins' son, daughter, son-in-law, and granddaughter. Many of their comments emphasized the victims' outstanding personal qualities, and noted how deeply the Bronsteins would be missed. Other parts of the VIS described the emotional and personal problems the family members have faced as a result of the crimes. The son, for example, said that he suffers from lack of sleep and depression, and is "fearful for the first time in his life." He said that in his opinion, his parents were "butchered like animals." The daughter said she also suffers from lack of sleep, and that since the murders she has become withdrawn and distrustful. She stated that she can no longer watch violent movies or look at kitchen knives without being reminded of the murders. The daughter concluded that she could not forgive the murderer, and that such a person could "[n]ever be rehabilitated." Finally, the granddaughter described how the deaths had ruined the wedding of another close family member that took place a few days after the bodies were discovered. Both the ceremony and the reception were sad affairs, and instead of leaving for her honeymoon, the bride attended the victims' funeral. The VIS also noted that the granddaughter had received counseling for several months after the incident, but eventually had stopped because she concluded that "no one could help her."

The DPP official who conducted the interviews concluded the VIS by writing:

"It became increasingly apparent to the writer as she talked to the family members that the murder of Mr. and Mrs. Bronstein is still such a shocking, painful, and devastating memory to them that it permeates every aspect of their daily lives. It is doubtful that they will ever be able to fully recover from this tragedy and not be haunted by the memory of the brutal manner in which their loved ones were murdered and taken from them."

Defense counsel moved to suppress the VIS on the ground that this information was both irrelevant and unduly inflammatory, and that therefore its use in a capital case violated the Eighth Amendment of the Federal Constitution. The Maryland trial court denied the motion, ruling that the jury was entitled to consider "any and all evidence which would bear on the [sentencing decision]." Booth's lawyer then requested that the prosecutor simply read the VIS to the jury rather than call the family members to testify before the jury. Defense counsel was concerned that the use of live witnesses would increase the inflammatory effect of the information. The prosecutor agreed to this arrangement.

The jury sentenced Booth to death for the murder of Mr. Bronstein and to life imprisonment for the murder of Mrs. Bronstein. On automatic appeal, the Maryland Court of Appeals affirmed [upheld] the conviction and the sentences. The court rejected Booth's claim that the VIS injected an arbitrary factor into the sentencing decision. The court noted that it had [previously] considered this argument . . . and concluded that a VIS serves an important interest by informing the sentencer of the full measure of harm caused by the crime. The Court of Appeals then examined the VIS in Booth's case, and concluded that it is a "relatively straightforward and factual description of the effects of these murders on members of the Bronstein family." It held that the death sentence had not been imposed under the influence of passion, prejudice, or other arbitrary factors.

We granted certiorari [agreed to hear the case] to decide whether the Eighth Amendment prohibits a capital sentencing jury from considering victim impact evidence. We conclude that it does, and now reverse.

It is well settled that a jury's discretion to impose the death sentence must be "suitably directed and limited so as to minimize the risk of wholly arbitrary and capricious action." Although this Court normally will defer to a state legislature's determination of what factors are relevant to the sentencing decision, the Constitution places some limits on this discretion. Specifically, we have said that a jury must make an "individualized determination" of whether the defendant [one charged with wrongdoing] in question should be executed, based on "the character of the individual and the circumstances of the crime." And while this Court has never said that the defendant's record, characteristics, and the circumstances of the crime are the only permissible sentencing considerations, a state statute that requires consideration of other factors must be scrutinized to ensure that the evidence has some bearing on the defendant's "personal responsibility and moral guilt." To do otherwise would create the risk that a death sentence will be based on considerations that are "constitutionally impermissible or totally irrelevant to the sentencing process."

The VIS in this case provided the jury with two types of information. First, it described the personal characteristics of the victims and the emotional impact of the crimes on the family. Second, it set forth the family members' opinions and characterizations of the crimes and the defendant. For the reasons stated below, we find that this information is irrelevant to a capital sentencing decision, and that its admission creates a constitutionally unacceptable risk that the jury may impose the death penalty in an arbitrary and capricious manner.

The greater part of the VIS is devoted to a description of the emotional trauma suffered by the family and the personal characteristics of the victims. The State claims that this evidence should be considered a "circumstance" of the crime because it reveals the full extent of the harm caused by Booth's actions. In the State's view, there is a direct, foreseeable nexus between the murders and the harm to the family, and thus it is not "arbitrary" for the jury to consider these consequences in deciding whether to impose the death penalty. Although "victim impact" is not an aggravating factor under Maryland law, the State claims that by knowing the extent of the impact upon and the severity of the loss to the family, the jury was better able to assess the "'gravity or aggravating quality'" of the offense.

While the full range of foreseeable consequences of a defendant's actions may be relevant in other criminal and civil contexts, we cannot agree that it is relevant in the unique circumstance of a capital sentencing hearing. In such a case, it is the function of the sentencing jury to "express the conscience of the community on the ultimate question of life or death." When carrying out this task the jury is required to focus on the defendant as a "uniquely individual human bein[g]." The focus of a VIS, however, is not on the defendant, but on the character and reputation of the victim and the effect on his family. These factors may be wholly unrelated to the blameworthiness of a particular defendant. As our cases have shown, the defendant often will not know the victim, and therefore will have no knowledge about the existence or characteristics of the victim's family. Moreover, defendants rarely select their victims based on whether the murder will have an effect on anyone other than the person murdered. Allowing the jury to rely on a VIS therefore could result in imposing the death sentence because of factors about which the defendant was unaware, and that were irrelevant to the decision to kill. This evidence thus could divert the jury's attention away from the defendant's background and record, and the circumstances of the crime.

It is true that in certain cases some of the information contained in a VIS will have been known to the defendant before he committed the offense. As we have recognized, a defendant's degree of knowledge of the probable consequences of his actions may increase his moral culpability in a constitutionally significant manner. We nevertheless find that because of the nature of the information contained in a VIS, it creates an impermissible risk that the capital sentencing decision will be made in an arbitrary manner.

As evidenced by the full text of the VIS in this case, the family members were articulate and persuasive in expressing their grief and the extent of their loss. But in some cases the victim will not leave behind a family, or the family members may be less articulate in describing their feelings even though their sense of loss is equally severe. The fact that the imposition of the death sentence may turn on such distinctions illustrates the danger of allowing juries to consider this information. Certainly the degree to which a family is willing and able to express its grief is irrelevant to the decision whether a defendant, who may merit the death penalty, should live or die. . . .

Nor is there any justification for permitting such a decision to turn on the perception that the victim was a sterling member of the community rather than someone of questionable character. This type of information does not provide a "principled way to distinguish [cases] in which the death penalty was imposed from the many cases in which it was not."

We also note that it would be difficult - if not impossible - to provide a fair opportunity to rebut such evidence without shifting the focus of the sentencing hearing away from the defendant. A threshold problem is that victim impact information is not easily susceptible to rebuttal. Presumably the defendant would have the right to cross-examine the declarants, but he rarely would be able to show that the family members have exaggerated the degree of sleeplessness, depression, or emotional trauma suffered. More-over, if the state is permitted to introduce evidence of the victim's personal qualities, it cannot be doubted that the defendant also must be given the chance to rebut this evidence. Putting aside the strategic risks of attacking the victim's character before the jury, in appropriate cases the defendant presumably would be permitted to put on evidence that the victim was of dubious moral character, was unpopular, or was ostracized from his family. The prospect of a "mini-trial" on the victim's character is more than simply unappealing; it could well distract the sentencing jury from its constitutionally required task - determining whether the death penalty is appropriate in light of the background and record of the accused and the particular circumstances of the crime. We thus reject the contention that the presence or absence of emotional distress of the victim's family, or the victim's personal characteristics, are proper sentencing considerations in a capital case.

The second type of information presented to the jury in the VIS was the family members' opinions and characterizations of the crimes. The Bronsteins' son, for example, stated that his parents were "butchered like animals," and that he "doesn't think anyone should be able to do something like that and get away with it." The VIS also noted that the Bronsteins' daughter

> "could never forgive anyone for killing [her parents] that way. She can't believe that anybody could do that to someone. The victims' daughter states that animals wouldn't do this. [The perpetrators] didn't have to kill because there was no one to stop them from looting. . . . The murders show the vicious-ness of the killers' anger. She doesn't feel that the people who did this could ever be rehabilitated and she doesn't want them to be able to do this again or put another family through this."

One can understand the grief and anger of the family caused by the brutal murders in this case, and there is no doubt that jurors generally are aware of these feelings. But the formal presentation of this information by the State can serve no other purpose than to inflame the jury and divert it from deciding the case on the relevant evidence concerning the crime and the defendant. As we have noted, any decision to impose the death sentence must "be, and appear to be, based on reason rather than caprice or emo-tion." The admission of these emotionally charged opinions as to what conclusions the jury should draw from the evidence clearly is inconsistent with the reasoned decisionmaking we require in capital cases.

We conclude that the introduction of a VIS at the sentencing phase of a capital murder trial violates the Eighth Amendment, and therefore the Maryland statute is invalid to the extent it re-quires consideration of this information. The decision of the Maryland Court of Appeals is vacated [annulled] to the extent that it affirmed the capital sentence. The case is remanded [returned] for further proceedings not inconsistent with this opinion.

Appendix: The Victim Impact Statement

"Mr. and Mrs. Bronstein's son, daughter, son-in-law, and grand-daughter were interviewed for purposes of the Victim Impact Statement. There are also four other grandchildren in the family. The victims' son reports that his parents had been married for fifty-three years and enjoyed a very close relationship, spending each day together. He states that his father had worked hard all his life and had been retired for eight years. He describes his mother as a woman who was young at heart and never seemed like an old lady. She taught herself to play bridge when she was in her seventies. The victims' son relates that his parents were amazing people who attended the senior citizens' center and made many devout friends. He indicates that he was very close to his parents, and that he talked to them every day. The victims' daughter also spent lots of time with them.

"The victims' son saw his parents alive for the last time on May 18th. They were having their lawn manicured and were excited by the onset of spring. He called them on the phone that evening and received no answer. He had made arrangements to pick Mr. Bronstein up on May 20th. They were both to be ushers in a granddaughter's wedding and were going to pick up their tuxedos. When he arrived at the house on May 20th he noticed that his parents' car wasn't there. A neighbor told him that he hadn't seen the car in several days and he knew something was wrong. He went to his parents' house and found them murdered. He called his sister crying and told her to come right over because something terrible had happened and their parents were both dead.

"The victims' daughter recalls that when she arrived at her parents' house, there were police officers and television crews everywhere. She felt numb and cold. She was not allowed to go into the house and so she went to a neighbor's home. There were people and reporters everywhere and all she could feel was cold. She called her older daughter and told her what had happened. She told her daughter to get her husband and then tell her younger daughter what had happened. The younger daughter was to be married two days later.

"The victims' granddaughter reports that just before she received the call from her mother she had telephoned her grandparents and received no answer. After her mother told her what happened she turned on the television and heard the news reports about it. The victims' son reports that his children first learned about their grandparents death from the television reports.

"Since the Jewish religion dictates that birth and marriage are more important than death, the granddaughter's wedding had to proceed on May 22nd. She had been looking forward to it eagerly, but it was a sad occasion with people crying. The reception, which normally would have lasted for hours, was very brief. The next day, instead of going on her honeymoon, she attended her grandparents' funerals. The victims' son, who was an usher at the wedding, cannot remember being there or coming and going from his parents' funeral the next day. The victims' granddaughter, on the other hand, vividly remembers every detail of the days following her grandparents' death. Perhaps she described the impact of the tragedy most eloquently when she stated that it was a completely devastating and life-altering experience.

"The victims' son states that he can only think of his parents in the context of how he found them that day, and he can feel their fear and horror. It was 4:00 p.m. when he discovered their bodies and this stands out in his mind. He is always aware of when 4:00 p.m. comes each day, even when he is not near a clock. He also wakes up at 4:00 a.m. each morning. The victims' son states that he suffers from lack of sleep. He is unable to drive on the streets that pass near his parents' home. He also avoids driving past his father's favorite restaurant, the supermarket where his parents shopped, etc. He is constantly reminded of his parents. He sees his father coming out of synagogues, sees his parents' car, and feels very sad whenever he sees old people. The victims' son feels that his parents were not killed, but were butchered like animals. He doesn't think anyone should be able to do something like that and get away with it. He is very angry and wishes he could sleep and not feel so depressed all the time. He is fearful for the first time in his life, putting all the lights on and checking the locks frequently. His children are scared for him and concerned for his health. They phone him several times a day. At the same time he takes a fearful approach to the whereabouts of his children. He also calls his sister every day. He states that he is frightened by his own reaction of what he would do if someone hurt him or a family member. He doesn't know if he'll ever be the same again.

"The victims' daughter and her husband didn't eat dinner for three days following the discovery of Mr. and Mrs. Bronstein's bodies. They cried together every day for four months and she still cries every day. She states that she doesn't sleep through a single night and thinks a part of her died too when her parents were killed. She reports that she doesn't find much joy in anything and her powers of concentration aren't good. She feels as if her brain is on overload. The victims' daughter relates that she had to clean out her parents' house and it took several weeks. She saw the bloody carpet, knowing that her parents had been there, and she felt like getting down on the rug and holding her mother. She wonders how this could have happened to her family because they're just ordinary people. The victims' daughter reports that she had become noticeably withdrawn and depressed at work and is now making an effort to be more outgoing. She notes that she is so emotionally tired because she doesn't sleep at night, that she has a tendency to fall asleep when she attends social events such as dinner parties or the symphony. The victims' daughter states that wherever she goes she sees and hears her parents. This happens every day. She cannot look at kitchen knives without being reminded of the murders and she is never away from it. She states that she can't watch movies with bodies or stabbings in it. She can't tolerate any reminder of violence. The victims' daughter relates that she used to be very trusting, but is not any longer. When the doorbell rings she tells her husband not to answer it. She is very suspicious of people and was never that way before.

"The victims' daughter attended the defendant's trial and that of the co-defendant because she felt someone should be there to represent her parents. She had never been told the exact details of her parents' death and had to listen to the medical examiner's report. After a certain point, her mind blocked out and she stopped hearing. She states that her parents were stabbed repeatedly with viciousness and she could never forgive anyone for killing them that way. She can't believe that anybody could do that to someone. The victims' daughter states that animals wouldn't do this. They didn't have to kill because there was no one to stop them from looting. Her father would have given them anything. The murders show the viciousness of the killers' anger. She doesn't feel that the people who did this could ever be rehabilitated and she doesn't want them to be able to do this again or put another family through this. She feels that the lives of her family members will never be the same again.

"The victims' granddaughter states that unless you experience something like this you can't understand how it feels. You are in a state of shock for several months and then a terrible depression sets in. You are so angry and feel such rage. She states that she only dwells on the image of their death when thinking of her grandparents. For a time she would become hysterical whenever she saw dead animals on the road. She is not able to drive near her grandparents' house and will never be able to go into their neighborhood again. The victims' granddaughter also has a tendency to turn on all the lights in her house. She goes into a panic if her husband is late coming home from work. She used to be an avid reader of murder mysteries, but will never be able to read them again. She has to turn off the radio or T.V. when reports of violence come on because they hit too close to home. When she gets a newspaper she reads the comics and throws the rest away. She states that it is the small everyday things that haunt her constantly and always will. She saw a counselor for several months but stopped because she felt that no one could help her.

"The victims' granddaughter states that the whole thing has been very hard on her sister too. Her wedding anniversary will always be bittersweet and tainted by the memory of what happened to her grandparents. This year on her anniversary she and her husband quietly went out of town. The victims' granddaughter finds that she is unable to look at her sister's wedding pictures. She also has a picture of her grandparents, but had to put it away because it was too painful to look at it.

"The victims' family members note that the trials of the suspects charged with these offenses have been delayed for over a year and the postponements have been very hard on the family emotionally. The victims' son notes that he keeps seeing news reports about his parents' murder which show their house and the police removing their bodies. This is a constant reminder to him. The family wants the whole thing to be over with and they would like to see swift and just punishment.

"As described by their family members, the Bronsteins were loving parents and grandparents whose family was most important to them. Their funeral was the largest in [the] history of the Levinson Funeral Home and the family received over one thousand sympathy cards, some from total strangers. They attempted to answer each card personally. The family states that Mr. and Mrs. Bronstein were extremely good people who wouldn't hurt a fly. Because of their loss, a terrible void has been put into their lives and every day is still a strain just to get through. It became increasingly apparent to the writer as she talked to the family members that the murder of Mr. and Mrs. Bronstein is still such a shocking, painful, and devastating memory to them that it permeates every aspect of their daily lives. It is doubtful that they will ever be able to fully recover from this tragedy and not be haunted by the memory of the brutal manner in which their loved ones were murdered and taken from them."

Protecting Children In Court
Maryland v. Craig

*The protection of minor victims of sex crimes from further trauma and em-
barrassment is a compelling one.*   **- Justice Sandra Day O'Connor**

In October 1986 Sandra Ann Craig, the owner of a nurs-
ery/kindergarten school located in Maryland's Howard County,
was indicted by a grand jury on charges of the sexual abuse of
children under her care. The only witnesses to her alleged abuse
were the children.

The Sixth Amendment's Confrontation Clause provides: "In all
criminal prosecutions, the accused shall enjoy the right . . . to be
confronted by the witnesses against them."

The State of Maryland, in an attempt to comply with the Confrontation Clause (while at the same time protecting children
from the trauma of having to testify in a courtroom, face-to-face
with their alleged abuser), enacted a "Child Testimony Law." The
law set up a procedure for hearing the testimony of a child via
one-way, closed-circuit television. In this procedure the alleged
sexual abuse victim testified in a separate room, in the presence
of only the prosecution and defense, while the judge, jury, and
defendant remained in the courtroom watching.

Craig's trial was conducted in accordance with Maryland's "Child
Testimony Law" and she was found guilty of the sexual abuse
charges. Arguing that the law violated her Confrontation Clause
right to face her accuser, Craig appealed to the Maryland Court
of Appeals, which reversed her conviction. Prosecutors appealed
this reversal to the United States Supreme Court.

On June 27, 1990 the 5-4 decision of the Supreme Court was
announced by Associate Justice Sandra Day O'Connor.

The *Craig* Court

Chief Justice William Rehnquist
Appointed Associate Justice by President Nixon
Appointed Chief Justice by President Reagan
Served 1971 -

Associate Justice William Brennan
Appointed by President Eisenhower
Served 1956 - 1990

Associate Justice Byron White
Appointed by President Kennedy
Served 1962 - 1993

Associate Justice Thurgood Marshall
Appointed by President Lyndon Johnson
Served 1967 - 1991

Associate Justice Harry Blackmun
Appointed by President Nixon
Served 1970 - 1994

Associate Justice John Paul Stevens
Appointed by President Ford
Served 1975 -

Associate Justice Sandra Day O'Connor
Appointed by President Reagan
Served 1981 -

Associate Justice Antonin Scalia
Appointed by President Reagan
Served 1986 -

Associate Justice Anthony Kennedy
Appointed by President Reagan
Served 1988 -

The complete text of *Maryland v. Craig* can be found in volume 497 of *United States Reports*. Our edited text follows.

MARYLAND v. CRAIG
June 27, 1990

JUSTICE SANDRA DAY O'CONNOR: This case requires us to decide whether the Confrontation Clause of the Sixth Amendment categorically prohibits a child witness in a child abuse case from testifying against a defendant [one charged with a crime] at trial, outside the defendant's physical presence, by one-way closed circuit television.

In October, 1986, a Howard County grand jury charged respondent [the party arguing against an appeal], Sandra Ann Craig, with child abuse, first and second degree sexual offenses, perverted sexual practice, assault, and battery. The named victim in each count was Brooke Etze, a six-year-old child who, from August, 1984, to June, 1986, had attended a kindergarten and prekindergarten center owned and operated by Craig.

In March, 1987, before the case went to trial, the State sought to invoke a Maryland statutory procedure that permits a judge to receive, by one-way closed circuit television, the testimony of a child witness who is alleged to be a victim of child abuse. To invoke the procedure, the trial judge must first determin[e] that testimony by the child victim in the courtroom will result in the child suffering serious emotional distress such that the child cannot reasonably communicate.

Once the procedure is invoked, the child witness, prosecutor, and defense counsel withdraw to a separate room; the judge, jury, and defendant remain in the courtroom. The child witness is then examined and cross-examined in the separate room, while a video monitor records and displays the witness' testimony to those in the courtroom. During this time, the witness cannot see the defendant. The defendant remains in electronic communication with defense counsel, and objections may be made and ruled on as if the witness were testifying in the courtroom.

In support of its motion invoking the one-way closed circuit television procedure, the State presented expert testimony that

Brooke, as well as a number of other children who were alleged to have been sexually abused by Craig, would suffer "serious emotional distress such that [they could not] reasonably communicate," if required to testify in the courtroom. . . .

Craig objected to the use of the procedure on Confrontation Clause grounds, but the trial court rejected that contention, concluding that, although the statute "take[s] away the right of the defendant to be face-to-face with his or her accuser," the defendant retains the "essence of the right of confrontation," including the right to observe, cross-examine, and have the jury view the demeanor of the witness. The trial court further found that, based upon the evidence presented . . . the testimony of each of these children in a courtroom will result in each child's suffering serious emotional distress . . . such that each of these children cannot reasonably communicate. The trial court then found Brooke and three other children competent to testify, and accordingly permitted them to testify against Craig via the one-way closed circuit television procedure. The jury convicted Craig on all counts, and the Maryland Court of Special Appeals affirmed [upheld] the convictions.

The Court of Appeals of Maryland reversed and remanded [returned the case to the lower court] for a new trial. The Court of Appeals rejected Craig's argument that the Confrontation Clause requires in all cases a face-to-face courtroom encounter between the accused and his accusers, but concluded: . . . the operative "serious emotional distress" which renders a child victim unable to "reasonably communicate" must be determined to arise, at least primarily, from face-to-face confrontation with the defendant. Thus, we construe [interpret] the phrase "in the courtroom" as meaning, for Sixth Amendment and [state constitution] confrontation purposes, "in the courtroom in the presence of the defendant." Unless prevention of "eyeball-to-eyeball" confrontation is necessary to obtain the trial testimony of the child, the defendant cannot be denied that right. . . . . We granted certiorari [agreed to hear the case] to resolve the important Confrontation Clause issues raised by this case.

The Confrontation Clause of the Sixth Amendment, made applicable to the States through the Fourteenth Amendment, provides: "In all criminal prosecutions, the accused shall enjoy the right . . . to be confronted with the witnesses against him."

We observed in *Coy v. Iowa* that "the Confrontation Clause guarantees the defendant a face-to-face meeting with witnesses appearing before the trier of fact [judge or jury]." This interpretation derives not only from the literal text of the Clause, but also from our understanding of its historical roots. We have never held, however, that the Confrontation Clause guarantees criminal defendants the *absolute* right to a face-to-face meeting with witnesses against them at trial. . . . The procedure challenged in *Coy* involved the placement of a screen that prevented two child witnesses in a child abuse case from seeing the defendant as they testified against him at trial. In holding that the use of this procedure violated the defendant's right to confront witnesses against him, we suggested that any exception to the right "would surely be allowed only when necessary to further an important public policy." . . . Because the trial court in this case made individualized findings that each of the child witnesses needed special protection, this case requires us to decide the question reserved [postponed] in *Coy*.

The central concern of the Confrontation Clause is to ensure the reliability of the evidence against a criminal defendant by subjecting it to rigorous testing in the context of an adversary proceeding before the trier of fact. . . .

[T]he right guaranteed by the Confrontation Clause includes not only a "personal examination," but also (1) insures that the witness will give his statements under oath - thus impressing him with the seriousness of the matter and guarding against the lie by the possibility of a penalty for perjury; (2) forces the witness to submit to cross-examination, the "greatest legal engine ever invented for the discovery of truth;" [and] (3) permits the jury that is to decide the defendant's fate to observe the demeanor of the witness in making his statement, thus aiding the jury in assessing his credibility.

The combined effect of these elements of confrontation - physical presence, oath, cross-examination, and observation of demeanor by the trier of fact - serves the purposes of the Confrontation Clause by ensuring that evidence admitted against an accused is reliable and subject to the rigorous adversarial testing that is the norm of Anglo-American criminal proceedings.

. . . . The law in its wisdom declares that the rights of the public shall not be wholly sacrificed in order that an incidental benefit may be preserved to the accused.

. . . [O]ur precedents [previous cases that are binding] establish that "the Confrontation clause reflects a *preference* for face-to-face confrontation at trial," a preference that "must occasionally give way to considerations of public policy and the necessities of the case." [W]e have attempted to harmonize the goal of the Clause - placing limits on the kind of evidence that may be received against a defendant - with a societal interest in accurate factfinding, which may require consideration of out-of-court statements.

We have accordingly interpreted the Confrontation Clause in a manner sensitive to its purposes and sensitive to the necessities of trial and the adversary process. Thus, though we reaffirm the importance of face-to-face confrontation with witnesses appearing at trial, we cannot say that such confrontation is an indispensable element of the Sixth Amendment's guarantee of the right to confront one's accusers. . . .

This interpretation of the Confrontation Clause is consistent with our cases holding that other Sixth Amendment rights must also be interpreted in the context of the necessities of trial and the adversary process. We see no reason to treat the face-to-face component of the confrontation right any differently, and indeed we think it would be anomalous to do so.

That the face-to-face confrontation requirement is not absolute does not, of course, mean that it may easily be dispensed with. As we suggested in *Coy*, our precedents confirm that a defendant's right to confront accusatory witnesses may be satisfied absent a physical, face-to-face confrontation at trial only where denial of such confrontation is necessary to further an important public policy and only where the reliability of the testimony is otherwise assured.

Maryland's statutory procedure, when invoked, prevents a child witness from seeing the defendant as he or she testifies against the defendant at trial. We find it significant, however, that Maryland's procedure preserves all of the other elements of the confrontation right: the child witness must be competent to testify and must testify under oath; the defendant retains full opportunity for contemporaneous cross-examination; and the judge, jury, and defendant are able to view (albeit by video monitor) the demeanor (and body) of the witness as he or she testifies. Although we are mindful of the many subtle effects face-to-face confrontation may have on an adversary criminal proceeding, the presence of these other elements of confrontation - oath, cross-examination, and observation of the witness' demeanor - adequately ensures that the testimony is both reliable and subject to rigorous adversarial testing in a manner functionally equivalent to that accorded live, in-person testimony. These safeguards of reliability and adversariness render the use of such a procedure a far cry from the undisputed prohibition of the Confrontation Clause: trial by *ex parte* [one-sided] affidavit [voluntary declaration under oath] or inquisition. Rather, we think these elements of effective confrontation not only permit a defendant to "confound and undo the false accuser, or reveal the child coached by a malevolent adult," but may well aid a defendant in eliciting favorable testimony from the child witness. . . . We are . . . confident that use of the one-way closed-circuit television procedure, where necessary to further an important state interest, does not impinge upon the truth-seeking or symbolic purposes of the Confrontation Clause.

The critical inquiry in this case, therefore, is whether use of the procedure is necessary to further an important state interest. The State contends that it has a substantial interest in protecting children who are allegedly victims of child abuse from the trauma of testifying against the alleged perpetrator, and that its statutory procedure for receiving testimony from such witnesses is necessary to further that interest.

We have of course recognized that a State's interest in "the protection of minor victims of sex crimes from further trauma and embarrassment" is a "compelling" one.

[W]e have sustained legislation aimed at protecting the physical and emotional wellbeing of youth even when the laws have operated in the sensitive area of constitutionally protected rights.

. . . . We . . . conclude today that a State's interest in the physical and psychological wellbeing of child abuse victims may be sufficiently important to outweigh, at least in some cases, a defendant's right to face his or her accusers in court. That a significant majority of States has enacted statutes to protect child witnesses from the trauma of giving testimony in child abuse cases attests to the wide-spread belief in the importance of such a public policy. Thirty-seven States, for example, permit the use of videotaped testimony of sexually abused children; 24 States have authorized the use of one-way closed circuit television testimony in child abuse cases; and 8 States authorize the use of a two-way system in which the child-witness is permitted to see the courtroom and the defendant on a video monitor and in which the jury and judge is permitted to view the child during the testimony.

The statute at issue in this case, for example, was specifically intended to safeguard the physical and psychological wellbeing of child victims by avoiding, or at least minimizing, the emotional trauma produced by testifying.

The *Wildermuth [v. State]* court noted: In Maryland, the Governor's Task Force on Child Abuse, in its *Interim Report*, documented the existence of the [child abuse] problem in our State. It brought the picture up to date in its *Final Report*. In the first six months of 1985, investigations of child abuse were 12 percent more numerous than during the same period of 1984. In 1979, 4,615 cases of child abuse were investigated; in 1984, 8,321. In its *Interim Report*, the Commission proposed legislation that, with some changes, became Section 9-102 [of the Maryland Code]. The proposal was aimed at alleviating the trauma to a child victim in the courtroom atmosphere by allowing the child's testimony to be obtained outside of the courtroom.

This would both protect the child and enhance the public interest by encouraging effective prosecution of the alleged abuser. Given the State's traditional and "'transcendent interest in protecting the welfare of children,'" and buttressed by the growing body of academic literature documenting the psychological trauma suffered by child abuse victims who must testify in court, we will not second-guess the considered judgment of the Maryland Legislature regarding the importance of its interest in protecting child abuse victims from the emotional trauma of testifying. Accordingly, we hold that, if the State makes an adequate showing of necessity, the state interest in protecting child witnesses from the trauma of testifying in a child abuse case is sufficiently important to justify the use of a special procedure that permits a child witness in such cases to testify at trial against a defendant in the absence of face-to-face confrontation with the defendant.

The requisite finding of necessity must, of course, be a case-specific one: the trial court must hear evidence and determine whether use of the one-way closed circuit television procedure is necessary to protect the welfare of the particular child witness who seeks to testify. The trial court must also find that the child witness would be traumatized, not by the courtroom generally, but by the presence of the defendant. Denial of face-to-face confrontation is not needed to further the state interest in protecting the child witness from trauma unless it is the presence of the defendant that causes the trauma. In other words, if the state interest were merely the interest in protecting child witnesses from courtroom trauma generally, denial of face-to-face confrontation would be unnecessary, because the child could be permitted to testify in less intimidating surroundings, albeit with the defendant present. Finally, the trial court must find that the emotional distress suffered by the child witness in the presence of the defendant is more than . . . "mere nervousness or excitement or some reluctance to testify." We need not decide the minimum showing of emotional trauma required for use of the special procedure, however, because the Maryland statute, which requires a determination that the child witness will suffer "serious emotional distress such that the child cannot reasonably communicate," clearly suffices to meet constitutional standards.

To be sure, face-to-face confrontation may be said to cause trauma for the very purpose of eliciting truth, but we think that the use of Maryland's special procedure, where necessary to further the important state interest in preventing trauma to child witnesses in child abuse cases, adequately ensures the accuracy of the testimony and preserves the adversary nature of the trial. Indeed, where face-to-face confrontation causes significant emotional distress in a child witness, there is evidence that such confrontation would in fact *disserve* the Confrontation Clause's truth-seeking goal.

In sum, we conclude that, where necessary to protect a child witness from trauma that would be caused by testifying in the physical presence of the defendant, at least where such trauma would impair the child's ability to communicate, the Confrontation Clause does not prohibit use of a procedure that, despite the absence of face-to-face confrontation, ensures the reliability of the evidence by subjecting it to rigorous adversarial testing and thereby preserves the essence of effective confrontation. Because there is no dispute that the child witnesses in this case testified under oath, were subject to full cross-examination, and were able to be observed by the judge, jury, and defendant as they testified, we conclude that, to the extent that a proper finding of necessity has been made, the admission of such testimony would be consonant with the Confrontation Clause.

. . . . So long as a trial court makes . . . a case-specific finding of necessity, the Confrontation Clause does not prohibit a State from using a one-way closed circuit television procedure for the receipt of testimony by a child witness in a child abuse case. Because the Court of Appeals held that the trial court had not made the requisite finding of necessity under its interpretation of "the high threshold required by [*Coy*] before [the Maryland Code] may be invoked," we cannot be certain whether the Court of Appeals would reach the same conclusion in light of the legal standard we establish today. We therefore vacate [annul] the judgment of the Court of Appeals of Maryland and remand the case for further proceedings not inconsistent with this opinion. It is so ordered.

Ineffective Counsel
Bell v. Cone

Without proof of both deficient performance and prejudice to the defense it could not be said that the sentence or conviction resulted from a breakdown in the adversary process that rendered the result of the proceeding unreliable.
- Chief Justice William Rehnquist

In August 1982 in Memphis, Tennessee, Gary Cone went on a two-day shooting rampage, which ended in the murder of an elderly couple. Tried in the Shelby County Criminal Court on two counts of first-degree murder, Cone was found guilty. In the penalty phase of the trial, the jury was to weigh the evidence and arguments and decide on either life imprisonment or a death sentence. The prosecution presented evidence of aggravating circumstances and, in closing argument, stressed the especially heinous nature of the murders. Cone's defense attorney, in contrast, presented no evidence of any mitigating circumstances and waived final argument. The jury sentenced Cone to death.

Cone contended that his Sixth Amendment right to effective assistance of counsel had been violated, and he appealed to the State's Criminal Appeals and Supreme Courts for a reversal of his death sentence. Both courts rejected his appeal. Cone filed a *habeus corpus* petition in U.S. District Court, demanding that Warden Bell be ordered to physically bring him to a federal court for a hearing of his ineffective assistance of counsel claim. The U.S. District Court denied this petition but, on appeal, the U.S. Court of Appeals found his Sixth Amendment rights had been violated and reversed the death sentence. Warden Bell appealed to the U.S. Supreme Court.

On May 28, 2002, the 8-1 decision of the Supreme Court was announced by Chief Justice William Rehnquist.

The *Cone* Court

Chief Justice William Rehnquist
Appointed Associate Justice by President Nixon
Appointed Chief Justice by President Reagan
Served 1971 -

Associate Justice John Paul Stevens
Appointed by President Ford
Served 1975 -

Associate Justice Sandra Day O'Connor
Appointed by President Reagan
Served 1981 -

Associate Justice Antonin Scalia
Appointed by President Reagan
Served 1986 -

Associate Justice Anthony Kennedy
Appointed by President Reagan
Served 1988 -

Associate Justice David Souter
Appointed by President Bush
Served 1990 -

Associate Justice Clarence Thomas
Appointed by President Bush
Served 1991 -

Associate Justice Ruth Bader Ginsberg
Appointed by President Clinton
Served 1993 -

Associate Justice Stephen Breyer
Appointed by President Clinton
Served 1994 -

The complete text of *Bell v. Cone* can be found in volume 535 of *United States Reports*. Our edited text follows.

BELL v. CONE
May 28, 2002

CHIEF JUSTICE WILLIAM REHNQUIST: The Tennessee
Court of Appeals rejected respondent [party arguing against an
appeal] [Gary Bradford Cone]'s claim that his counsel rendered
ineffective assistance during his sentencing hearing under
principles announced in *Strickland* v. *Washington*. The Court of
Appeals for the Sixth Circuit concluded that *United States* v. *Cronic*
should have controlled the state court's analysis and granted him
a conditional writ of habeas corpus [an order to bring an issue to
the court]. We hold that [Cone]'s claim was governed by
Strickland, and that the state court's decision neither was
"contrary to" nor involved "an unreasonable application of
clearly established Federal law." . . .

In 1982, [Cone] was convicted of, and sentenced to death for, the
murder of an elderly couple in Memphis, Tennessee. The killings
culminated a 2-day crime rampage that began when [Cone]
robbed a Memphis jewelry store of approximately $112,000 in
merchandise on a Saturday in August 1980. Shortly after the
12:45 p.m. robbery, a police officer in an unmarked vehicle
spotted [Cone] driving at a normal speed and began to follow
him. After a few blocks, [Cone] accelerated, prompting a high-
speed chase through midtown Memphis and into a residential
neighborhood where [Cone] abandoned his vehicle. Attempting
to flee, [Cone] shot an officer who tried to apprehend him, shot a
citizen who confronted him, and, at gunpoint, demanded that
another hand over his car keys. As a police helicopter hovered
overhead, [Cone] tried to shoot the fleeing car owner, but was
frustrated because his gun was out of ammunition. Throughout
the afternoon and into the next morning, [Cone] managed to
elude detection as police combed the surrounding area. In the
meantime, officers inventorying his car found an array of illegal
and prescription drugs, the stolen merchandise, and more than
$2,400 in cash. [Cone] reappeared early Sunday morning when he
drew a gun on an elderly resident who refused to let him in to
use her telephone. Later that afternoon, [Cone] broke into the
home of Shipley and Cleopatra Todd, aged 93 and 79 years old,

and killed them by repeatedly beating them about the head with a blunt instrument. He moved their bodies so that they would not be visible from the front and rear doors and ransacked the first floor of their home. After shaving his beard, [Cone] traveled to Florida. He was arrested there for robbing a drugstore in Pompano Beach. He admitted killing the Todds and shooting the police officer.

A Tennessee grand jury charged [Cone] with two counts of first-degree murder in the perpetration of a burglary in connection with the Todds' deaths, three counts of assault with intent to murder in connection with the shootings and attempted shooting of the car owner, and one count of robbery with a deadly weapon for the jewelry store theft. At a jury trial in the Criminal Court of Shelby County, the prosecution adduced [offered] overwhelming physical and testimonial evidence showing that [Cone] perpetrated [committed] the crimes and that he killed the Todds in a brutal and callous fashion. The defense conceded that [Cone] committed most of the acts in question, but sought to prove that he was not guilty by reason of insanity. A clinical psychologist testified that [Cone] suffered from substance abuse and post-traumatic stress disorders related to his military service in Vietnam. A neuropharmacologist recounted at length [Cone]'s history of illicit drug use, which began after he joined the Army and escalated to the point where he was daily consuming "rather horrific" quantities. That drug use, according to the expert, caused chronic amphetamine psychosis, hallucinations, and ongoing paranoia, which affected [Cone]'s mental capacity and ability to obey the law. Defense counsel also called [Cone]'s mother, who spoke of her son coming back from Vietnam in 1969 a changed person, his honorable discharge from service, his graduation with honors from college, and the deaths of his father and fiancée while he was in prison from 1972 - 1979 for robbery. Although [Cone] did not take the stand, defense counsel was able to elicit through other testimony that he had expressed remorse for the killings. Rejecting his insanity defense, the jury found him guilty on all charges.

Punishment for the first-degree murder counts was fixed in a separate sentencing hearing that took place the next day and lasted about three hours. Under then-applicable Tennessee law, a death sentence was required if the jury found unanimously that the State proved beyond a reasonable doubt the existence of at least one statutory aggravating circumstance [tending to increase the penalty] that was not outweighed by any mitigating circumstance [tending to lessen the penalty]. In making these determinations, the jury could (and was instructed that it could) consider evidence from both the guilt and punishment phases.

During its opening statement, the State said it would prove four aggravating factors: that (1) [Cone] had previously been convicted of one or more felonies involving the use or threat of violence to a person; (2) he knowingly created a great risk of death to two or more persons other than the victim during the act of murder; (3) the murder was especially heinous, atrocious, or cruel; and (4) the murder was committed for the purpose of avoiding [a lawful] arrest. In his opening statement, defense counsel called the jury's attention to the mitigating evidence already before them. He suggested that [Cone] was under the influence of extreme mental disturbance or duress, that he was an addict whose drug and other problems stemmed from the stress of his military service, and that he felt remorse. Counsel urged the jury that there was a good reason for preserving his client's life if one looked at "the whole man." He asked for mercy, calling it a blessing that would raise them above the State to the level of God. The prosecution then called a records custodian and fingerprint examiner to establish that [Cone] had three armed robbery convictions and two officers who said they tried unsuccessfully to arrest [Cone] for armed robbery after the jewelry store heist. Through cross-examination of the records custodian, [Cone]'s attorney brought out that his client had been awarded the Bronze Star in Vietnam. After defense counsel successfully objected to the State's proffer of photos of the Todds' decomposing bodies, both sides rested. The junior prosecuting attorney on the case gave what the state courts described as a "low-key" closing. Defense counsel waived final argument, preventing the lead prosecutor, who by all accounts was an extremely effective advocate, from arguing in rebuttal [contrary argument]. The jury found in both murder cases four aggravating factors and no mitigating circumstances substantial enough to outweigh them. The Tennessee Supreme Court

138 Criminal Justice Decisions

affirmed [upheld] [Cone]'s convictions and sentence on appeal, and we denied certiorari [hearing the case].

[Cone] then petitioned for state postconviction relief, contending that his counsel rendered ineffective assistance during the sentencing phase by failing to present mitigating evidence and by waiving final argument. After a hearing in which [Cone]'s trial counsel testified, a division of the Tennessee Criminal Court rejected this contention. The Tennessee Court of Criminal Appeals affirmed. The appellate court reviewed counsel's explanations for his decisions concerning the calling of witnesses and the waiving of final argument. Describing counsel's representation as "very conscientious," the court concluded that his performance was within the permissible range of competency, citing *Baxter* v. *Rose*, a decision the Tennessee Supreme Court deems to have announced the same attorney performance standard as *Strickland* v. *Washington*. The court also expressed its view that [Cone] received the death penalty based on the law and facts, not on the shortcomings of counsel. The Tennessee Supreme Court denied [Cone] permission to appeal, and we denied further review.

In 1997, after his second application for state postconviction relief was dismissed, [Cone] sought a federal writ of habeas corpus under [the U.S. Code] as amended by the Antiterrorism and Effective Death Penalty Act of 1996. His petition alleged [claimed] numerous grounds for relief including ineffective assistance at the sentencing phase. The District Court ruled that [Cone] did not meet [the U.S. Code]'s requirements and denied the petition. The Court of Appeals affirmed the refusal to issue a writ with respect to [Cone]'s conviction, but reversed with respect to his sentence. It held that [Cone] suffered a Sixth Amendment violation for which prejudice should be presumed under *United States* v. *Cronic*, because his counsel, by not asking for mercy after the prosecutor's final argument, did not subject the State's call for the death penalty to meaningful adversarial testing. The state court's adjudication [judgment given] of [Cone]'s Sixth Amendment claim, in the Court of Appeals' analysis, was therefore an unreasonable application of the clearly established law announced in *Strickland*. We [agreed to hear the case], and now reverse the Court of Appeals.

The Antiterrorism and Effective Death Penalty Act of 1996 modified a federal habeas court's role in reviewing state prisoner applications in order to prevent federal habeas "retrials" and to ensure that state-court convictions are given effect to the extent possible under law. To these ends, [the U.S. Code] provides:

"(d) An application for a writ of habeas corpus on behalf of a person in custody pursuant to the judgment of a State court shall not be granted with respect to any claim that was adjudicated on the merits [legal rights of the parties] in State court proceedings unless the adjudication of the claim - "(1) resulted in a decision that was contrary to, or involved an unreasonable application of, clearly established Federal law, as determined by the Supreme Court of the United States."

As we stated in *Williams*, [the U.S. Code]'s "contrary to" and "unreasonable application" clauses have independent meaning. A federal habeas court may issue the writ under the "contrary to" clause if the state court applies a rule different from the governing law set forth in our cases, or if it decides a case differently than we have done on a set of materially indistinguishable [the same] facts. The court may grant relief under the "unreasonable application" clause if the state court correctly identifies the governing legal principle from our decisions but unreasonably applies it to the facts of the particular case. The focus of the latter inquiry is on whether the state court's application of clearly established federal law is objectively unreasonable, and we stressed in *Williams* that an unreasonable application is different from an incorrect one.

Petitioner [one who brings an appeal to the court] [Bell] contends that the Court of Appeals exceeded its statutory authority to grant relief under [the U.S. Code] because the decision of the Tennessee courts was neither contrary to nor an unreasonable application of the clearly established law of *Strickland*. [Cone] counters that he is entitled to relief under [the U.S. Code]'s "contrary to" clause because the state court applied the wrong legal rule. In his view, *Cronic*, not *Strickland*, governs the analysis of his claim that his counsel rendered ineffective assistance at the sentencing hearing. We address this issue first.

In *Strickland*, which was decided the same day as *Cronic*, we announced a two-part test for evaluating claims that a defendant's [one charged with a crime] counsel performed so incompetently in his or her representation of a defendant that the defendant's sentence or conviction should be reversed. We reasoned that there would be a sufficient indication that counsel's assistance was defective enough to undermine confidence in a proceeding's result if the defendant proved two things: first, that counsel's "representation fell below an objective standard of reasonableness"; and second, that "there is a reasonable probability that, but for counsel's unprofessional errors, the result of the proceeding would have been different." Without proof of both deficient performance and prejudice to the defense, we concluded, it could not be said that the sentence or conviction "resulted from a breakdown in the adversary process that rendered the result of the proceeding unreliable," and the sentence or conviction should stand. In *Cronic*, we considered whether the Court of Appeals was correct in reversing a defendant's conviction under the Sixth Amendment without inquiring into counsel's actual performance or requiring the defendant to show the effect it had on the trial. We determined that the court had erred and remanded [returned to the lower court] to allow the claim to be considered under *Strickland*'s test. In the course of deciding this question, we identified three situations implicating the right to counsel that involved circumstances "so likely to prejudice the accused that the cost of litigating their effect in a particular case is unjustified."

First and "[m]ost obvious" was the "complete denial of counsel." A trial would be presumptively unfair, we said, where the accused is denied the presence of counsel at "a critical stage," a phrase we used in *Hamilton* v. *Alabama*, and *White* v. *Maryland*, to denote a step of a criminal proceeding, such as arraignment [court appearance to enter a plea], that held significant consequences for the accused. Second, we posited that a similar presumption was warranted if "counsel entirely fails to subject the prosecution's case to meaningful adversarial testing." Finally, we said that in cases like *Powell* v. *Alabama*, where counsel is called upon to render assistance under circumstances where competent counsel very likely could not, the defendant need not show that the proceedings were affected.

[Cone] argues that his claim fits within the second exception identified in *Cronic* because his counsel failed to "mount some case for life" after the prosecution introduced evidence in the sentencing hearing and gave a closing statement. We disagree. When we spoke in *Cronic* of the possibility of presuming prejudice based on an attorney's failure to test the prosecutor's case, we indicated that the attorney's failure must be complete. We said "if counsel *entirely* fails to subject the prosecution's case to meaningful adversarial testing." Here, [Cone]'s argument is not that his counsel failed to oppose the prosecution throughout the sentencing proceeding as a whole, but that his counsel failed to do so at specific points. For purposes of distinguishing between the rule of *Strickland* and that of *Cronic*, this difference is not of degree but of kind. The aspects of counsel's performance challenged by [Cone] - the failure to adduce mitigating evidence and the waiver of closing argument - are plainly of the same ilk as other specific attorney errors we have held subject to *Strickland*'s performance and prejudice components. In *Darden* v. *Wainwright*, for example, we evaluated under *Strickland* a claim that counsel was ineffective for failing to put on any mitigating evidence at a capital sentencing [where the death penalty may be imposed] hearing. In *Burger* v. *Kemp*, we did the same when presented with a challenge to counsel's decision at a capital sentencing hearing not to offer any mitigating evidence at all. We hold, therefore, that the state court correctly identified the principles announced in *Strickland* as those governing the analysis of [Cone]'s claim. Consequently, we find no merit in [Cone]'s contention that the state court's adjudication was contrary to our clearly established law.

The remaining issue, then, is whether [Cone] can obtain relief on the ground that the state court's adjudication of his claim involved an "unreasonable application" of *Strickland*. In *Strickland* we said that "[j]udicial scrutiny of a counsel's performance must be highly deferential" and that "every effort [must] be made to eliminate the distorting effects of hindsight, to reconstruct the circumstances of counsel's challenged conduct, and to evaluate the conduct from counsel's perspective at the time." Thus, even when a court is presented with an ineffective-assistance claim not subject to [the U.S. Code] deference, a defendant must overcome the "presumption that, under the circumstances, the challenged action 'might be considered sound trial strategy.'" For [Cone] to succeed, however, he must do more than show that he would have satisfied *Strickland*'s test if his claim were being analyzed in the first instance, because under [the U.S. Code], it is not enough to convince a federal habeas court that, in its independent judgment, the state-court decision applied *Strickland* incorrectly. Rather, he must show that the Tennessee Court of Appeals applied *Strickland* to the facts of his case in an objectively unreasonable manner. This, we conclude, he cannot do. [Cone]'s counsel was faced with the formidable task of defending a client who had committed a horribly brutal and senseless crime against two elderly persons in their home. He had just the day before shot a police officer and an unarmed civilian, attempted to shoot another person, and committed a robbery. The State had near conclusive proof of guilt on the murder charges as well as extensive evidence demonstrating the cruelty of the killings. Making the situation more onerous were the facts that [Cone], despite his high intelligence and relatively normal upbringing, had turned into a drug addict and had a history of robbery convictions.

Because the defense's theory at the guilt phase was not guilty by reason of insanity, counsel was able to put before the jury extensive testimony about what he believed to be the most compelling mitigating evidence in the case - evidence regarding the change his client underwent after serving in Vietnam; his drug dependency, which apparently drove him to commit the robbery in the first place; and its effects. Before the state courts, [Cone] faulted his counsel for not recalling his medical experts during the sentencing hearing. But we think counsel reasonably could have concluded that the substance of their testimony was still fresh to the jury. Each had taken the stand not long before, and counsel focused on their testimony in his guilt phase closing argument, which took place the day before the sentencing hearing was held. [Cone]'s suggestion that the jury could not fully consider the mental health proof as potentially mitigating because it was adduced during the guilt phase finds no support in the record. Defense counsel advised the jury that the testimony of the experts established the existence of mitigating circumstances, and the trial court specifically instructed the jury that evidence of a mental disease or defect insufficient to establish a criminal defense could be considered in mitigation. [Cone] also assigned error in his counsel's decision not to recall his mother. While counsel recognized that [Cone]'s mother could have provided further information about [Cone]'s childhood and spoken of her love for him, he concluded that she had not made a good witness at the guilt stage, and he did not wish to subject her to further cross-examination. [Cone] advances no argument that would call his attorney's assessment into question.

In his trial preparations, counsel investigated the possibility of calling other witnesses. He thought [Cone]'s sister, who was closest to him, might make a good witness, but she did not want to testify. And even if she had agreed, putting her on the stand would have allowed the prosecutor to question her about the fact that [Cone] called her from the Todds' house just after the killings. After consulting with his client, counsel opted not to call [Cone] himself as a witness. And we think counsel had sound tactical reasons for deciding against it. [Cone] said he was very angry with the prosecutor and thought he might lash out if pressed on cross-examination, which could have only alienated him in the eyes of the jury. There was also the possibility of calling other witnesses from his childhood or days in the Army. But counsel feared that the prosecution might elicit information about [Cone]'s criminal history. He further feared that testimony about [Cone]'s normal youth might, in the jury's eyes, cut the other way.

[Cone] also focuses on counsel's decision to waive final argument. He points out that counsel could have explained the significance of his Bronze Star decoration and argues that his counsel's failure to advocate for life in closing necessarily left the jury with the impression that he deserved to die. The Court of Appeals "reject[ed] out of hand" the idea that waiving summation could ever be considered sound trial strategy. In this case, we think at the very least that the state court's contrary assessment was not "unreasonable." After [Cone]'s counsel gave his opening statement discussing the mitigating evidence before them and urging that they choose life for his client, the prosecution did not put on any particularly dramatic or impressive testimony. The

State's witnesses testified rather briefly about the undisputed facts that [Cone] had prior convictions and was evading arrest.

When the junior prosecutor delivered a very matter-of-fact closing that did not dwell on any of the brutal aspects of the crime, counsel was faced with a choice. He could make a closing argument and reprise for the jury, perhaps in greater detail than his opening, the primary mitigating evidence concerning his client's drug dependency and posttraumatic stress from Vietnam. And he could plead again for life for his client and impress upon the jurors the importance of what he believed were less significant facts, such as the Bronze Star decoration or his client's expression of remorse. But he knew that if he took this opportunity, he would give the lead prosecutor, who all agreed was very persuasive, the chance to depict his client as a heartless killer just before the jurors began deliberation. Alternatively, counsel could prevent the lead prosecutor from arguing by waiving his own summation and relying on the jurors' familiarity with the case and his opening plea for life made just a few hours before. Neither option, it seems to us, so clearly outweighs the other that it was objectively unreasonable for the Tennessee Court of Appeals to deem counsel's choice to waive argument a tactical decision about which competent lawyers might disagree.

We cautioned in *Strickland* that a court must indulge a "strong presumption" that counsel's conduct falls within the wide range of reasonable professional assistance because it is all too easy to conclude that a particular act or omission of counsel was unreasonable in the harsh light of hindsight. Given the choices available to [Cone]'s counsel and the reasons we have identified, we cannot say that the state court's application of *Strickland*'s attorney-performance standard was objectively unreasonable. The judgment of the Court of Appeals is therefore reversed, and the case is remanded for further proceedings consistent with this opinion. It is so ordered.

BIBLIOGRAPHY

Adler, Freda, Gerhard O.W. Mueller, and William S. Laufer. *Criminal Justice: An Introduction*. New York, NY: McGraw-Hill, 1999.

Agresto, John. *The Supreme Court and Constitutional Democracy*. Ithaca, NY: Cornell University Press, 1984.

Baker, Liva. *Miranda: Crime, Law, and Politics*. New York, NY: Atheneum, 1983.

Banaszak, Ronald, Editor. *Fair Trial Rights of the Accused: A Documentary History*. Westport, CT: Greenwood Press, 2002.

Beaney, William Merritt. *The Right to Counsel in American Courts*. Westport, CT: Greenwood Press, 1972.

Bodenhamer, David J. *Fair Trial: Rights of the Accused in American History*. New York, NY: Oxford University Press, 1992.

Cheatham, Elliott Evans. *A Lawyer When Needed*. New York, NY: Columbia University Press, 1963.

Cook, Joseph G. *Constitutional Rights of the Accused: Post-Trial Rights*. Rochester, NY: Lawyers Cooperative Publishing Co., 1976.

Cox, Archibald. *The Court and the Constitution*. New York, NY: Houghton-Mifflin, 1988.

Davis, Mark S. *Concise Dictionary of Crime and Justice*. Thousand Oaks, CA: Sage Publications, 2002.

Freedman, Warren. *The Constitutional Right to a Speedy and Fair Criminal Trial*. New York, NY: Quorum Books, 1989.

Friedman, Lawrence Meir. *Crime and Punishment in American History*. New York, NY: Basic Books, 1994.

Ginger, Ann Fagan. *The Law, The Supreme Court, and The People's Rights.* Woodbury, NY: Barron's Educational Series, 1973.

Goode, Stephen. *The Controversial Court: Supreme Court Influences on American Life.* New York, NY: Messner, 1982.

Gora, Joel M. *Due Process of Law.* Skokie, IL: National Textbook Co., 1977.

Hall, Kermit L., Editor. *The Rights of the Accused: The Justices and Criminal Justice.* New York, NY: Garland Pub., 2000.

Harr, J. Scott, and Karen M. Hess. *Constitutional Law and the Criminal Justice System.* Florence, KY: Wadsworth Publishing Co., 2001.

Hermann, Robert, Eric Single, and John Boston. *Counsel For the Poor: Criminal Defense in Urban America.* Lexington, MA: Lexington Books, 1977.

Leahy, James E. *Liberty, Justice, and Equality: How These Constitutional Guarantees Have Been Shaped by United States Supreme Court Decisions Since 1789.* Jefferson, NC: McFarland & Co., 1992.

Leighton, Paul, and Jeffrey Reiman, Editors. *Criminal Justice Ethics.* Upper Saddle River, NJ: Pearson Education, 2000.

Leo, Richard A., and George C. Thomas III, Editors. *The Miranda Debate: Law, Justice, and Policing.* Boston, MA: Northeastern University Press, 1998.

Lewis, Anthony. *Clarence Earl Gideon and the Supreme Court.* New York, NY: Random House, 1972.

_____. *Gideon's Trumpet.* Birmingham, AL: Notable Trials Library, 1991.

_____. *The Supreme Court and How It Works: The Story of the Gideon Case.* New York, NY: Random House, 1966.

Lewis, Peter W., and Kenneth D. Peoples. *The Supreme Court and the Criminal Process: Cases and Comments.* Philadelphia, PA: Saunders, 1978.

McDonald, William F., Editor. *The Defense Counsel.* Beverly Hills, CA: Sage Publications, 1983.

McGehee, Lucius Polk. *Due Process of Law Under the Federal Constitution.* Littleton, CO: F.B. Rothman, 1980.

Pennock, J. Roland, and John W. Chapman, Editors. *Due Process.* New York, NY: New York University Press, 1977.

Rehnquist, William H. *The Supreme Court: How It Was, How It Is.* New York, NY: Morrow, 1987.

Rush, George E. *Dictionary of Criminal Justice.* New York, NY: McGraw-Hill, 1999.

Scalia, John. *Federal Pretrial Release and Detention.* Washington, DC: U.S. Department of Justice, 1999.

Sigler, Jay A. *Double Jeopardy: The Development of a Legal and Social Policy.* Ithaca, NY: Cornell University Press, 1969.

Stevens, Leonard A., *Death Penalty: The Case of Life vs. Death in the United States.* New York, NY: Coward, McCann & Geoghegan, 1978.

_____. *Trespass!: The People's Privacy vs. The Power of the Police.* New York, NY: Coward, McCann & Geoghegan, 1977.

Thomas, George C. *Double Jeopardy: The History, The Law.* New York, NY: New York University Press, 1998.

Umbreit, Mark S., Robert B. Coates, and Boris Kalanj. *Victim Meets Offender: The Impact of Restorative Justice and Mediation.* Monsey, NY: Criminal Justice Press, 1994.

Walker, Samuel, and T. Stuart Walker. *Popular Justice: A History of American Criminal Justice*. New York, NY: Oxford University Press, 1997.

Way, H. Frank. *Criminal Justice and the American Constitution*. North Scituate, MA: Duxbury Press, 1980.

Wilkes, Daniel. *Post-Conviction Constitutional Rights of Indigent Defendants: State Interpretations of* Griffin v. Illinois. New York, NY: The Institute, 1959.

Woodward, Bob, and Scott Armstrong. *The Brethren: Inside the Supreme Court*. New York, NY: Simon & Schuster, 1979.

📖 EXCELLENT BOOKS ORDER FORM 📖

(Please xerox this form so it will be available to other readers.)

Please send the following books:

___ Criminal Justice Decisions
___ Death Penalty Decisions
___ Landmark American Speeches: The 17th & 18th Centuries
___ Landmark American Speeches: The 19th Century
___ Landmark American Speeches: The 20th Century
___ Landmark Decisions of the U.S. Supreme Court I
___ Landmark Decisions of the U.S. Supreme Court II
___ Landmark Decisions of the U.S. Supreme Court III
___ Landmark Decisions of the U.S. Supreme Court IV
___ Landmark Decisions of the U.S. Supreme Court V
___ Landmark Decisions of the U.S. Supreme Court VI
___ Freedom of Speech Decisions
___ Freedom of the Press Decisions
___ Freedom of Religion Decisions
___ Civil Rights Decisions: The 19th Century
___ Civil Rights Decisions: The 20th Century
___ Obscenity & Pornography Decisions
___ Schoolhouse Decisions
___ Life, Death, and the Law

- -

All Excellent Books are $19.95 each.
Order directly from us for a discount.
Add $2.00 shipping/handling for the first book
and $1.00 each for every other book ordered.

Name: _____

Organization: _____

Address: _____

E-mail: _____ Fax: _____

City: _____ State: ____ Zip: _____

Send your check or purchase order to:
Excellent Books, POB 131322, Carlsbad, CA 92013-1322;
Phone: **760-598-5069**; Fax: **240-218-7601**;
E-mail: **books@excellentbooks.com**;
or visit our website at **excellentbooks.com**